Cross Country
Ski Areas:
A Critical Guide

Cross Country Ski Areas: A Critical Guide

THE BEST OF NEW ENGLAND'S TOURING CENTERS

Raymond Elman

THE STEPHEN GREENE PRESS
PELHAM BOOKS

THE STEPHEN GREENE PRESS/PELHAM BOOKS

Published by the Penguin Group
Viking Penguin, a division of Penguin Books USA Inc., 375 Hudson Street,
   New York, New York 10014, U.S.A.
Penguin Books Ltd., 27 Wrights Lane, London W8 5T2, England
Penguin Books Australia Ltd, Ringwood, Victoria, Australia
Penguin Books Canada Ltd, 2801 John Street, Markham, Ontario, Canada
   L3R 1B4
Penguin Books (N.Z.) Ltd, 182-190 Wairau Road, Auckland 10, New
Zealand

Penguin Books Ltd, Registered Offices: Harmondsworth, Middlesex, England

First published in 1987 by The Stephen Greene Press/Pelham Books
This revised edition published in 1990
Distributed by Viking Penguin, a division of Penguin Books USA Inc.

10 9 8 7 6 5 4 3 2 1

Copyright © The Stephen Greene Press Inc., 1987
Copyright © Penguin Books USA Inc., 1990
All rights reserved

Maps on pages 19, 51, 65, and 101 are by the author.
All other maps are originally by Northern Cartographic, with revisions by Karen
Shea. Maps for ski areas in Vermont first appeared in *Vermont Cross-Country Ski
Atlas;* used with permission.

Library of Congress Cataloging-in-Publication Data
Elman, Raymond.
   Cross country ski areas : a critical guide : the best of New England's
touring centers / by Raymond Elman.
         p.   cm.
      ''Pelham Books.''
      Rev. ed. of: Critical guide to cross-country ski areas. 1987.
      ISBN 0-8289-0808-7
      1. Cross-country skiing—New England—Directories. 2. Ski resorts—
New England—Directories. I. Elman, Raymond. Critical guide to cross-
country ski areas. II. Title.
GV854.5.N35E46   1990
796.93'2—dc20   9032969
                                                                            CIP
Printed in the United States of America
Set in Futura and Goudy Old Style by Publication Services, Inc.
Designed by Deborah Schneider
Produced by Unicorn Production Services, Inc.

To my wife, Lee,
who skied every kilometer with me,
and then some;
and to my new son Evan,
for the trails ahead

Contents

Vermont

Weather Phones:

MAINE	207/496-8931
WESTERN MASSACHUSETTS	413/499-2627
NEW HAMPSHIRE	603/225-3161
VERMONT	802/862-2475

Acknowledgments

This project is deeply indebted to Tom and Deborah Begner, the people who put me on my first pair of skinny skis despite my obstinate protests that I hated the cold, I hated the idea of being wet and cold, and that my art career could not sustain another sports addiction. Although they never dreamed that their innocent invitation to ski with them in Vermont could so totally transform the patterns of my life (I became an instant cross country ski fanatic), they have generously continued to foster my addiction by sharing the hospitality of their winter abode and by suggesting I write this book.

This project was fortunate to receive contributions from John Dostal, Andrew Nemethy, Mike Farny, Galen Sayward, and Craig Woods, all of whose many years of experience in the sport were extremely valuable in shaping the approach and contents of this guide.

In addition, I would like to acknowledge the technical and equipment support of Salomon North America, Järvinen USA, Fischer of America, Inc., and Excel, Inc.

The publishers would also like to thank Northern Cartographic of Burlington, Vermont, and Karen Shea, for creating the trail maps for this book.

Introduction

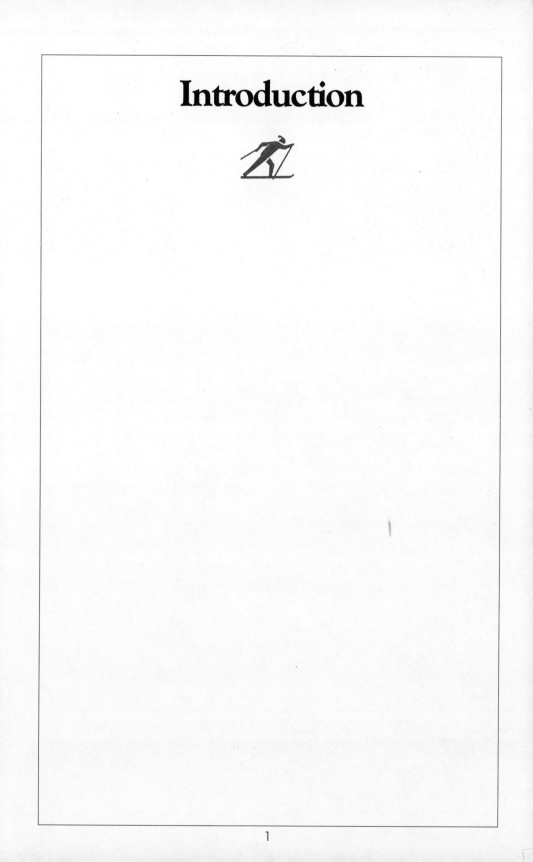

Why Do You Need This Guide?

You're perusing the available cross country ski literature (state-sponsored tourist pamphlets, magazines, guidebooks), looking for a new place to ski. One cross country ski center, within a reasonable 2½- to 3-hour drive from home, keeps appearing in all the right places. It offers 40 km of trails, it's located in a quintessentially charming New England village renowned for a wide variety of dining establishments, and if you tire of skiing, it boasts other divertissements such as a complete sports facility, Jacuzzis, saunas, sleigh rides, sophisticated boutiques, and live entertainment. So you call the local chamber of commerce, obtain a list of hostelries in the area, and make a series of long-distance calls until you find an inn that isn't fully reserved for the next three months.

The long-anticipated ski weekend in February finally arrives. Unable to sleep, you rise at 6:30 A.M. and try to communicate your enthusiasm to your bleary-eyed family. You and your wife pack the kids, the baby-sitter, the skis, poles, and boots, the tennis gear, the extra blankets, and six suitcases stuffed with an adequate supply of ski clothes to develop the "layered look" into your Saab and head for the mountains. You arrive at the inn by 10:00 A.M. Everything is just as you'd pictured it: a smallish, neatly trimmed, converted Victorian farmhouse, with a foot of snow on the roof, elongated icicles dripping from the eaves, the smell of burning wood emanating from the chimney, and everywhere the bustle of winter enthusiasts preparing for a robust day on the ski trails.

As quickly as possible, you check into your room, dump all of the gear, and help everyone get appropriately outfitted for a Nordic experience. You head over to the cross country ski center, enroll the kids in a special day-long children's ski program, and eagerly approach an impossibly healthy-looking ski instructor for advice on trail conditions, wax selection, and recommended loops for skiers of your ability. "Well, the trails are a little icy today," he says, "but if you can ski beyond Sven's

Pasture to Heartattack Hill, the conditions improve."
You say to yourself, just because I look out of shape, he
probably thinks he's talking to a novice—the weather
conditions have been favorable; the trails can't be all
that bad.

So you chart a course to Sven's Pasture, cork in the
recommended kick wax, and push off. The beginning of
the trail is a gentle downhill. Not too bad, you think, nice
glide. But the gentle downhill soon bottoms out in a
shallow valley, and then you have to go up. Slip, slip,
slide, slip, plop. No grip, no kick. So you try skating—
same thing, you can't get an edge to bite. The whole
trail system is a solid block of ice! You're at the bottom
of a hill, and you can't go forward or backward. When
you dreamed of a weekend of cross country skiing, you
never imagined this scenario.

What's the Problem? The problem is that the ski center that looked so promising on paper has not invested
in advanced grooming equipment. They do not possess
a power tiller to break up the ice and convert it into a
skiable surface.

Has This Ever Happened to You?

You and your in-laws plan a weekend cross country ski
getaway. You see an ad in your hometown newspaper
for a ski "chalet" for rent at reasonable rates, and it is
near both Alpine and Nordic skiing areas. The cross
country ski center has 60 km of trails that connect five
inns. The trail system was designed by a well-known ski
center manager who has since moved on to make
another area famous.

On Friday afternoon, you and the in-laws leave work
early to gather baggage, kids, and animals and get a
head start on the Washington's Birthday traffic. But you
are not alone; the interstate is jammed with similarly
loaded vehicles. The recognition factor is terrifying. So
your winter getaway is transformed into a trudge. By the
time you exit from the interstate, a snowstorm has developed, and your two cars warily continue along pitch-
black country roads toward your rented ski "chalet."

The directions for the final 10-mile, off-highway approach to your rented abode are slightly vague, so you
become vaguely lost—two sets of in-laws bumping

around in the dark. By 10:00 P.M. the rented ski "chalet" is finally illuminated by your headlights. Your group stumbles wearily from the vehicles and enters the dark dwelling. You hear a low gurgling noise that reminds you of a gentle brook. As you step through the doorway, you discover two inches of water covering the floor. Opening other doors and flicking switches, you also learn that the heating system has gone south with the plumbing.

Happy Washington's Birthday. You eventually find George, the caretaker of the ski chalet, at an all-night poker game. Reluctantly (he is ahead), George leaves the game to rescue you by telephoning the owner of another identical ski "chalet" and persuading him to allow you sanctuary. Though all of the water in your new resting spot is securely frozen in the pipes, in the sink, and in the toilet, at least the heating unit satisfyingly rumbles into operation. George assures that the frozen water will thaw without cracking the pipes, and—too tired to argue—you accept this information and retire.

Unbelievably, the next day breaks sunny and gorgeous. The pipes are still intact, the toilet flushes, and seasoned logs crackle in the wood stove. Your thoughts turn from survival to skiing.

After a hearty skier's breakfast, you and your group divide up into Nordics and Alpiners. The Nordics drive over to the cross country ski center and begin to reconnoiter. The trail map illustrates a system that matches expectations: 60 km of trails, varying elevations, five inns connected to the network. So you ask the fellow behind the desk for advice on which inn makes the best lunch destination, what trails provide the most enjoyable route, and the wax of the hour. He tells you. You tell the group. Before the adventure begins, you notice a few things that seem a little out of character for a major ski center: the wax supplies are meager, they've run out of wax remover, the rental equipment is a mélange of outdated models, and none of the other skiers appears to be as good as you are.

Nevertheless, the sky is without clouds, the sun is warm, and you envision a beautiful day of striding and gliding to lunch. Disappointment, however, is not far away. As soon as you begin to ski up out of the valley where the ski shop is nestled, the suggested wax of the hour becomes the glue of the moment. So all of the wax lovers have to break and rearrange their klister. Once the striding and gliding have recommenced, the quality of trail grooming begins to deteriorate. The farther away from the ski shop you go, the less evidence there is that someone has passed by with a grooming machine. But you've broken trail before, so undaunted, you continue in search of lunch.

Unfortunately, ungroomed trails eventually become unmaintained trails. There are bushes growing in the middle of the trail! And now you're headed downhill! You try to ski bowlegged and straddle the bushes, but you can't help but notice the tug of twigs on the sheer Lycra between your legs. There is only one way to preserve your outer layer. So you stop at the first opportunity, remove your skis, and start walking, hoping that this is only a temporary situation.

What's the Problem? The problem is a lack of dedicated management. The trails are there, the terrain is good, the grooming equipment is excellent, but no one cares.

Or, Has This Ever Happened To You?

Every time you've stopped at the last state-sponsored information center and toilet facility on your way home from one of your favorite ski areas, you've noticed promotional material about a cross country ski center and connected inn that are a lot closer to your home. Finally, you read somewhere that the mystery ski center (you never hear of anyone who has skied there) has joined ranks with a neighboring system and increased its trail network to 60 km of excellent skiing.

So one weekend, when you weren't allowed to head up early to ski country because you had to make a mandatory appearance at a cocktail party, you decide to make a day trip to the new-and-improved mystery ski center.

As you approach the ski center and notice the abundance of fresh powder, you begin to fantasize about the skiing possibilities only 90 minutes from home. If this place is as good as its pamphlets, you've discovered a very convenient spot for a "ski fix" to tide you over till the next big getaway.

You park the Saab and begin to absorb some of the local details. Flags from a variety of world-class ski countries flutter above the inn and the ski shop, projecting a feeling of international flair and a racer's-edge, state-of-the-art, championship-caliber approach to skiing. But as your eye drifts down from the majestic banners to the edifices they adorn, you notice that all of the buildings bear the unmistakable marks of quick-buck investors (cheap construction masquerading as Saint-Moritz).

Forewarned, you walk into the ski shop. Uh, oh! The ski shop—with low ceilings, green Astroturf carpet, and open space begging for a Ping-Pong table—looks like a suburban basement "rec" room. Where is all the ski equipment? You talk to the manager, a fresh-faced kid from Colorado. He launches into a litany of financial mumbo jumbo about a recent change in the corporate infrastructure of the ski facility.

Swell, but how are the trails? He hands you a trail map. Yes, 60 km of trails are schematically represented on the trail map. Unfortunately, despite the abundance of fresh powder, he has managed to groom only 10 km of the easiest trails.

Some people claim to have climbed Mount Everest because "it was there." Borrowing that sound bit of philosophy, you decide to ski what the ski area has provided. You unpack the skinny skis and give it a go. Boring! So you put the skis back on the roof rack, and consult a map in search of another cross country ski center. Unbelievably, you find one less than 50 miles away. How long would it take Stirling Moss to get there, you wonder, as you speed away from the financial quagmire.

What's the Problem? The problem is that you didn't use the telephone. If you have to do any significant traveling in search of skiable tracks, you can save yourself lots of aggravation by calling ahead and asking very specific questions. What are the snow conditions? Powder? Icy? Corn snow? How many kilometers are open and are groomed? How many kilometers have been groomed in the past 24 hours? How many kilometers of "most difficult" trails are open?

Do any of these stories strike a familiar note? They sound like "Ol' Man River" to us! Anyone who approaches cross country skiing as a nomad (searches for the area with the best snow conditions each week instead of specializing in one region of New England) will eventually develop a diary of the characteristics of each ski center—which centers honestly describe snow conditions over the telephone, which can provide good skiing during marginal conditions, which trails are fun to ski again and again, where the best après-ski facilities are located, and so forth and so on.

Treat this guidebook as your instant, personal ski diary, with all of the trial and error removed. In an orderly, systematic manner, we've done all of your legwork. As we compiled the results of our XC center reviews, a clear picture of the New England Nordic-skiing industry developed, and we realized that there was an upper class of cross country ski centers in this region, conveniently distributed throughout a four-state area. So we decided to focus on only the best XC centers in New England, and as a result, we feel confident recommending any ski center that we have included in this book.

In the following section, we explain how the book was assembled, some of the criteria for inclusion, definitions of key terms and categories, and recommended ways for using this guide to plan pleasurable cross country skiing adventures. Though we are well aware of the almost irresistible temptation to ignore this introduction and head straight for our review of your favorite ski area, you have purchased this book for our advice— and our first piece of advice is read the next section first.

A Guide to the Guidebook

You can't travel very long in ski country during a meager snow season without hearing the locals complain that city dwellers don't think about skiing unless they look out the window and see snow. This was especially true during the snow droughts of the early 1980s. As Bostonians who did not own or rent a ski house, we were initially victims of the snow drought. We would telephone friends who were lucky enough to possess dwellings in ski country and try to persuade them that they would enjoy their skiing more if they invited us to participate, only to hear that snow conditions were terrible. At first we knew only of the ski areas frequented by our friends, so we either skied with them or didn't ski at all. Sometimes during those lean years we would arrive at their local ski area only to discover that the trails were in terrible shape, and the experience would be transformed from a winter delight into a heart-in-your-throat nightmare.

Gradually, we weaned ourselves from relying on our friends and began to develop a list of cross country ski centers all over New England that we could call in search of the optimum snow conditions for a given weekend ski trip. We learned which ski areas had high-quality grooming equipment and knew how to use it, who would honestly describe the trail conditions over the telephone, and which XC centers had the most enjoyable trail systems. As a result, during the particularly lean winters of 1983–1985 and 1988–1989, while our friends were complaining that their ski season was ruined, we skied all over New England without missing a week.

In this guidebook, we offer in-depth information to help you choose among the best cross country ski centers in New England.

The Method We assembled a panel of experienced cross country skiers (including ski writers Craig Woods, John Dostal, and Andrew Nemethy, ski coach Galen Sayward, and editor Tom Begner) to discuss the type of ski-area information that would be most useful to our readers. We decided that we wanted to avoid creating a "chamber of commerce" book—the type that praises the good points of each area until they all begin to sound alike and dissolve into a swirl of quaint New England charm, hearty soups, roaring fires, hardwood forests, and Alpine vistas. We arbitrarily decided that we would consider only those ski centers that had at least 25 km of trails.

Having defined our target, we developed a standard, detailed questionnaire to provide a structure for comparing one area to another. We asked questions that had not been asked by other guidebooks: what kind of grooming equipment do you use? Who grooms your trails? A skier? A farmer? Do you rent racing skis? How many kilometers do you groom for skating? Where is the best sauna in town?

Armed with our intimidating questionnaire, our reviewers crisscrossed New England. It soon became apparent that there was a creme rising to the top of our survey. Cross country skiers have become much more demanding: they want high-quality grooming, intelligently cut trails, skating trails, good rental equipment, and après-ski amenities. Meeting such demands requires a substantial investment of capital, time, and energy, and many of the ski areas on our review list simply didn't cut the mustard. One area operator, who maintains 40 km of trails, complained to us that he was going out of business because the old-timers who had supported him over the years had been replaced by a new breed of skiers who thumbed their noses at the quality of his trails. We decided that rather than criticize ski areas for failing to keep up with the demands of contemporary skiers, we would focus on the cross country ski centers that were manifestly dedicated to staying abreast of developments in the sport through constant improvement. Though our list dwindled to 32 ski areas, we still found worthy XC centers in all regions of New England.

Review Categories

Our comments on each of the cross country ski centers are in a standard format. The following explanations of some of the categories (the rest are self-explanatory) will help you compare and contrast the reviews.

TRAILS: In this category we have tried to give you a feel for the length, nature, and degree of difficulty of each trail system. Since it was not practical for us to actually measure each trail network, we have relied on the information reported by the ski areas. We have also used their degree-of-difficulty designations. Trail length and degree-of-difficulty designations have always been terms of contention. Though some XC centers actually measure their trails, others estimate their distances. We often hear claims that some centers advertise artificial trail lengths as a marketing device. We also hear complaints that what is considered "more difficult" at one ski center is "easiest" at another. This arena of debate will never be resolved, and we need not enter it. We believe that all of the XC centers included in this book have enough kilometers of trails to keep you entertained for a weekend and sufficient challenges to satisfy your thirst for thrills. The centers included in this book represent a broad variety of skiing philosophies as well. There are wide, impeccably groomed trails appealing to racers and skaters, trails with a tinge of rusticity for those who prefer civilized, backcountry skiing, trails designed with young families in mind, trails that seem to go on forever, and long downhill runs for those who yearn for the thrill of the Alpine sport without the annoyance of lift lines.

As for trail maps, we believe that for safety purposes they should at least report the length and degree of difficulty of each trail. The better trail maps are printed on waterproof paper and are accurate, rather than schematic, representations; contain contour lines or indicate the direction of slopes; and offer descriptions of each trail or suggested trail sequences for skiers of differing abilities. We were astounded by the varying quality of the XC center trail maps. Approximately half of the cross country ski centers in this book do not offer maps that indicate trail length, and some of the maps were of such poor quality as to be almost useless.

To help you understand some of our comments on specific trails and obtain a general impression of the design of each trail network, we have included a map of the trail system of each XC center. However, it is possible that some of these maps are not up-to-date, since the better ski areas tend to adjust and add trails every year. Given the extreme variety of trail-map design we encountered, we hired Northern Cartographic, Inc., an experienced mapmaking concern in Burlington, Vermont, to homogenize the design of each map so that you would have a more uniform basis for comparison.

Be aware that the maps included in this book are *not* substitutes for the maps available at the XC centers, since trails change on a regular basis, but *do* give you a reasonably good means of comparison and contrast.

GROOMING: Generally, two types of machines are used for pulling grooming equipment: the Pisten Bully and the snowmobile. When we refer to state-of-the-art grooming equipment, we are always referring to a Pisten Bully capable of pulling a power tiller, the best device for breaking up icebound trails. Although snowmobiles and the Pisten Bully can both be used to create excellent trails during good snow conditions, during marginal conditions the Pisten Bully is clearly superior. The one drawback to a Pisten Bully is that the trails have to be wide enough to accommodate its girth, and we sometimes hear complaints that Pisten Bully-groomed trails are about as romantic as an interstate highway. It is also worth noting, however, that wide, well-groomed trails (e.g., steep downhill sections rolled smooth to facilitate snowplowing) are safer.

FOOD & LODGING: This book is not intended to be a substitute for a guide to country inns and restaurants. Though we begged our publisher to cough up enough expense money to field-test every attractive inn and eatery, he was adamant that we stick to the point—skiing. The establishments that we recommend in this section are the product of experience and hot tips. We assure you that there are plenty of cozy, charming inns and delicious dining spots that we have never visited.

Each ski area has special character traits that enhance the memorable quality of a Nordic sojourn. You can choose between sophisticated cuisine with a matching price tag and food cut to a logger's diet; quaint old New England inns and sleek new condominiums with all of the latest sensual accoutrements (saunas, whirlpool, massage); food cooked in trailside cabins and fast foods frozen in California and microwaved to suit your palate.

GESTALT: In this section we have attempted to give you a subjective feeling for the whole by commenting on some of the parts.

The reviews also include discussion of Alpine facilities near the cross country ski center for those who enjoy both skinny skis and metal edges, and the types of lessons available at each facility. For those haunted by images of themselves injured and abandoned in the middle of nowhere, we describe the safety features at each area. We also include information on childcare facilities, races, tours, special events, and other sport possibilities (e.g., tennis, squash, ice-skating, racquetball, swimming).

Terms We Use

Throughout the guidebook we will use phrases and terms that warrant some explanation at the outset.

Skating. This relatively new ski technique burst onto the American scene with the surprising success of Bill Koch. In skating, kick wax is ignored and the entire ski is glide-waxed. The skier glides from side to side rather than skiing in tracks. The inherent conflict between skating and diagonal stride initially caused havoc for most XC centers because a group of skaters could obliterate set tracks. When skating was first introduced, the number of practitioners was limited to a few racers, but the quantity of skaters has increased dramatically in the last few years, forcing the XC center operators to develop solutions to the conflict. Some areas have set aside trails for skating that are rolled but not tracked. Many areas have widened their trails to accommodate the side-to-side motion of skating and have created trails wide enough to contain both a set of tracks and a skating surface.

Skaters beware! Skating trails are not cast in concrete. We have observed that some of the trails that we were allowed to skate in December were double tracked and deemed "off limits to skaters" in January. This lack of a firm skating policy is a reflection of the XC center operators' ambivalent posture toward accommodating skaters.

So if you are committed to skating, call the cross country ski center before embarking and confirm the nature of the trails that are available for your purposes.

Traditional or Classic Technique. With the advent of skating, ski writers felt compelled to develop new terminology to describe the diagonal stride. In this book, when we use the terms *traditional* or *classic technique* we are always referring to the diagonal stride.

Lycra Set. Lycra, a stretch synthetic fabric, has become like a second skin for many skiers. Once worn only by racers, the flashy look and high-tech performance of this miracle fabric has attracted less talented skiers as well. When we refer to the Lycra set, however, we are talking about ski racers, and often we are commenting on the demands of skiers who skate.

Traditionalists. Classic-style skiers who wouldn't be caught dead in Lycra. Prefer leisurely skiing to racing, striding to skating.

Connected to the Catamount Trail. The Catamount Trail is a partially completed route that stretches from Quebec to Massachusetts along the ridgeline of Vermont's Green Mountains, linking 22 established XC centers, 11 of which are included in this guidebook. Although much of the 280-mile route is already accessible to skiers in the form of groomed XC center trails, unplowed roads, and other public trails, there are undeveloped sections that remain to be approved and cleared. For additional information, write to The Catamount Trail Association, P.O. Box 897, Burlington, Vermont 05402.

Locating the Best Place to Ski

All of the cross country ski centers included in this book provide enough kilometers of trails to keep anyone entertained for at least one day, so the first consideration in selecting one of these XC centers is the snow conditions. Don't be afraid to make a number of long-distance telephone calls and don't be afraid to consider areas that are a few miles farther north than you normally like to travel. Sometimes an extra hour spent on the phone and behind the wheel can mean the difference between skiing fresh powder and skiing reconstituted ice.

Start with the weather reports published in most newspapers. Notice the temperature ranges over the last few days. If the thermometer has hovered around freezing in the more southern regions of ski country, then XC centers in those areas are more likely to have icy conditions. Check reports of recently fallen snow. Many areas will require a couple of days to groom a foot of fresh powder, while a two-inch dusting could mean ideal ski conditions. Once you have narrowed your focus to a few regions, call for local weather reports using the telephone numbers provided on the contents page.

Some newspapers (e.g., *The Boston Globe*) routinely publish Alpine ski reports in their sports section. Use these reports as a guide to ski conditions at XC centers, remembering that most Alpine areas also produce artificial snow.

Other sources of information are state-sponsored tourist-information centers and industry-sponsored cross country ski reports. Methods of obtaining this information tend to vary from year to year, but we have usually found that each year at least one such report is available over the telephone. To obtain these telephone numbers will require a little research on your part.

When you have selected likely candidates for a great day of skiing, call the chosen cross country ski centers and, using some of the information available in this book, ask very pointed questions:

* *How many kilometers are open for skiing?*
* *How many of the most difficult trails are open?* Ask this question even if you are a beginner, because if most of the difficult trails are open, you can feel assured that the easier trails are in good condition, and that a large crowd of skiers will be dispersed over the whole trail network.
* *What wax are they using?* Even if you use waxless skis you should ask about the wax. If they are using klister, either the snow is old or the trail system has been subjected to a period of above and below freezing temperatures.
* *How are the roads?* Certain areas sustain long periods of bad driving conditions even if there has not been a recent snowstorm. A ski trip that doubles in driving time because of poor road conditions can pound a solid stake in the heart of any weekend.

- *Are they expecting a crowd?* If the center anticipates swarms of skiers, you should consider getting an earlier-than-anticipated start.

- *Do you need to reserve rental equipment?* You should know what size skis, boots, and poles you require; if you don't know, you can obtain these measurements at your local ski shop.

If New England is having a good snow season, you are likely to develop a large list of candidates for your ski dollar. Remember that planning pays off. The best way to enjoy cross country skiing is to ski great trails during good conditions. If you can remain flexible in choosing a destination, and put a little effort into selecting the cross country ski center with the best trail conditions, you will increase the likelihood of experiencing a season of memorable skiing.

Legend for Trail Maps

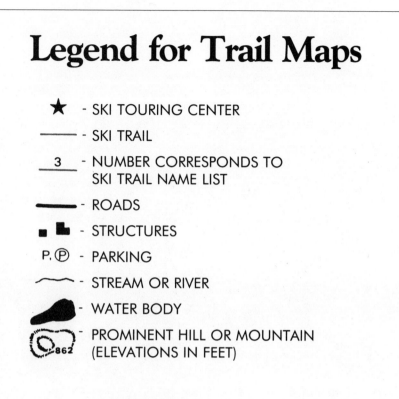

★ - SKI TOURING CENTER

—— - SKI TRAIL

<u>3</u> - NUMBER CORRESPONDS TO
SKI TRAIL NAME LIST

— - ROADS

▪ ▙ - STRUCTURES

P.Ⓟ - PARKING

〰 - STREAM OR RIVER

⬬ - WATER BODY

◉862 - PROMINENT HILL OR MOUNTAIN
(ELEVATIONS IN FEET)

TRAIL RATINGS

● EASIER

▪ MORE DIFFICULT

◆ MOST DIFFICULT

1 KM = .62 MILES

Maine

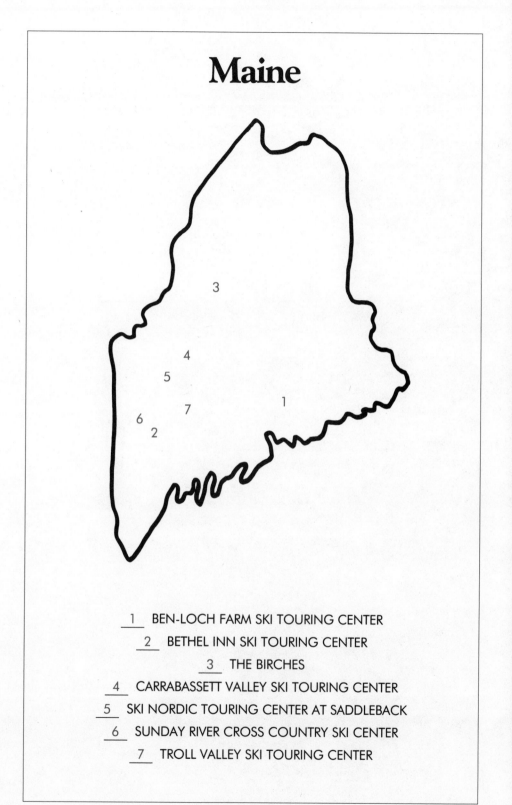

1	BEN-LOCH FARM SKI TOURING CENTER
2	BETHEL INN SKI TOURING CENTER
3	THE BIRCHES
4	CARRABASSETT VALLEY SKI TOURING CENTER
5	SKI NORDIC TOURING CENTER AT SADDLEBACK
6	SUNDAY RIVER CROSS COUNTRY SKI CENTER
7	TROLL VALLEY SKI TOURING CENTER

Ben-Loch Farm Ski Touring Center

R.F.D. 1, BOX 1020, NORTH ROAD
DIXMONT, MAINE 04932

For Ski Conditions:

HOURS OF OPERATION: 10:00 A.M. to dusk, daily

SNOW PHONE: 207/257-4768

Profile:

TRAILS: Ben-Loch has 16 trails, totaling approximately 35 km, all of which are groomed and track set as needed. Some of the more advanced trails are groomed for skating, including Kenduskeag (7.6 km) and Sheepscot (4.3 km). Most of the trails can be skied in one direction only. The trail system is classified as 11 percent easy, 65 percent more difficult, and 24 percent most difficult.

GROOMING: Above average. Ben-Loch uses a Bombardier, but they do not possess a powder maker to groom during frozen conditions. Though in our experience of this area we have always been satisfied with the quality of the grooming, we still recommend that you call ahead if you suspect icy conditions.

RENTALS: Ben-Loch rents a wide variety of equipment, including Järvinen, Atomic, Åsnes, and Epoke waxless and waxable skis, mounted with SNS and 75-mm bindings, and mated with Salomon, Alfa, Jalas, and Merrell boots. Although they sell racing skis, they do not rent them. They also have two pairs of snowshoes.

FOR WAX LOVERS: A complete supply of wax accessories is available. One waxes in a comfortable, heated basement, where there are lockers, workbenches, and electrical outlets.

FOOD & LODGING: The Lodge at Ben-Loch Farm provides all of the creature comforts that most of us would need in a cross country environment. The lodge offers single, double, and group rooms (with and without private bath), most of which have been recently built and are tastefully furnished.

The lodge has recently added a complete dining facility (breakfast, brunch, and dinner) featuring an

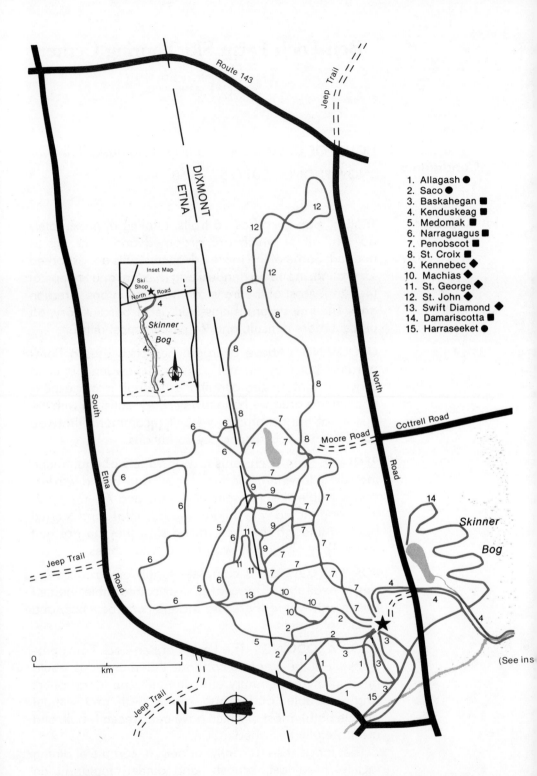

Route 143

Jeep Trail

DIXMONT
ETNA

Inset Map

Ski Shop
North   Road

4

Skinner
Bog

4

4

N

South

Etna

Road

Jeep Trail

1. Allagash ●
2. Saco ●
3. Baskahegan ■
4. Kenduskeag ■
5. Medomak ■
6. Narraguagus ■
7. Penobscot ■
8. St. Croix ■
9. Kennebec ◆
10. Machias ◆
11. St. George ◆
12. St. John ◆
13. Swift Diamond ◆
14. Damariscotta ■
15. Harraseeket ●

North

Cottrell Road

Moore Road

Road

Skinner

Bog

(See ins

0   1
km

Jeep Trail

N

eclectic array of taste treats ranging from kippered herring to bouillabaisse to smoked Cornish hen.

Should you desire other culinary adventures, there are many restaurants in the nearby (20-mile radius) towns of Newport, Bangor, and Carmel.

ALPINE FACILITIES IN AREA: Hermon Mountain, Eaton Mountain.

LESSONS: Instruction is available in all traditional cross country skiing techniques. They also maintain a Nordic-skiing library and have instructive video tapes to help polish your skills.

SAFETY: The trails are patrolled by members of the Maine Nordic Ski Patrol, and there is an end-of-the-day trail sweep. They also use a mobile, on-trail, ranger-communication system.

CHILDCARE FACILITIES: None.

Gestalt:

Ben-Loch Farm exists for cross country skiing. It is not a four-season inn that tossed in an XC trail network as an inducement to winter travelers. At Ben-Loch the ski center came first, then the inn.

The trail network winds through the Dixmont Hills and provides several vistas. This trail system offers truly memorable skiing for skiers of all levels.

Advanced beginners in good condition and intermediate skiers will enjoy the Kenduskeag Trail, with its gently rolling hills winding through Skinner Bog. This trail is 7.6 km each way (15.2 km total), so don't bite off more than you can ski.

Although we could recommend several advanced trails for downhill thrills and tight turns, we suggest you try the new-and-improved, 4.3-km Sheepscot Trail.

If the names of these trails strike a familiar note, it's because all of the trails are named after Maine rivers.

Let's hear some applause for the trail map. It's well designed and easy to read, contains all necessary information (including contour lines), and provides a detailed scenic and degree-of-difficulty description of each trail.

Extras: RACES: Ben-Loch hosts one race each year in the Maine Nordic Council Ski Series, as well as several biathlon events.

SPECIAL EVENTS: Night skiing with head lamps, clinics.

Travel Instructions: FROM BOSTON: Follow I-95 north to exit 42 between Newport and Bangor, Maine. Take Route 143 east for about 3½ miles, turn right at the Ben-Loch sign onto North Road, and continue for 1½ miles to the XC center.

FROM NEW YORK: Take I-95 north. Proceed as outlined above.

All of the roads are usually well maintained.

2

Bethel Inn Ski Touring Center

P.O. BOX 49
BETHEL, MAINE 04217

For Ski Conditions:

HOURS OF OPERATION: 8:30 A.M. to 5 P.M., daily

SNOW PHONE: 207/824-2175

Profile:

TRAILS: Bethel Inn has 14 trails, totaling approximately 33 km, all of which are groomed; 25 km are track set. Skating is permitted on the 8 km of rolled trails; many of the other trails are too narrow for skating. The trail system is classified as 40 percent easy, 40 percent more difficult, and 20 percent most difficult.

GROOMING: Above average. Though the Bethel Inn does not possess state-of-the-art grooming equipment, they were able to provide excellent skiing on the same day that the trails of another XC center in the region (with superior equipment) were soft.

RENTALS: Trak is their brand: waxless skis, boots, bindings, and poles. They do not rent waxable skis or racing skis. But they do rent pulkas for those parents who enjoy dragging their kids along the trails.

FOR WAX LOVERS: A complete supply of wax accessories is available. The downstairs section of the inn doubles as a golf clubhouse and the ski center headquarters. Waxing is permitted in this heated facility.

FOOD & LODGING: Bethel has a number of inns, bed-and-breakfasts, and restaurants from which to choose. The entire town has been designated a National Historic District, and after a fresh coating of snow, Bethel can fulfill anyone's expectations of how a classic New England village should look.

And you don't have to look any farther than the Bethel Inn for a classic, reasonably priced place to stay. Their brochure alerts us that the inn is comprised of several buildings—"a village of elegant colonial architecture." In fact, Hallmark chose one of the inn's buildings to grace a Christmas greeting card.

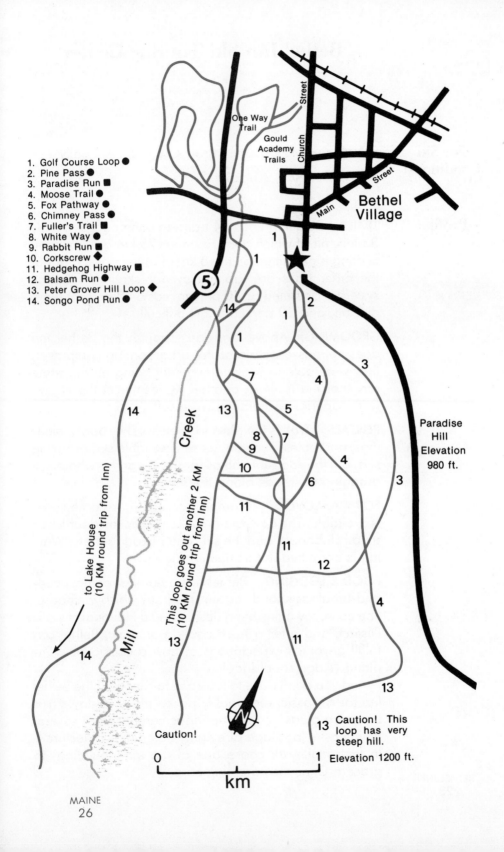

1. Golf Course Loop ●
2. Pine Pass ●
3. Paradise Run ■
4. Moose Trail ●
5. Fox Pathway ●
6. Chimney Pass ●
7. Fuller's Trail ■
8. White Way ●
9. Rabbit Run ■
10. Corkscrew ◆
11. Hedgehog Highway ■
12. Balsam Run ●
13. Peter Grover Hill Loop ◆
14. Songo Pond Run ●

One Way Trail

Gould Academy Trails

Church Street

Main Street

Bethel Village

Paradise Hill Elevation 980 ft.

Creek

Mill

to Lake House (10 KM round trip from Inn)

This loop goes out another 2 KM (10 KM round trip from Inn)

Caution!

Caution! This loop has very steep hill.
Elevation 1200 ft.

0   1

km

ALPINE FACILITIES IN AREA: Sunday River, Mount Abram.

LESSONS: Instruction is available in all methods of cross country skiing.

SAFETY: There are sporadic trail patrols during the day, but no trail sweeps at the end of the day. There is a sign-in–sign-out system.

CHILDCARE FACILITIES: Baby-sitting is available with advance notice.

Gestalt:

Though the town of Bethel is rarely mentioned in the same sentences that laud Stowe and Jackson, Bethel boasts two enjoyable ski centers (Bethel Inn and Sunday River, combined trail system of 70 km) and surely demands consideration as one of the better places to ski in New England.

We skied the Bethel Inn system the day after skiing a more renowned XC center in the region, and the pleasure we found in skiing the inn's narrow trails reminded us of the contrasts and trade-offs inherent in the wide trails designed to accommodate skating and the beauty of skiing more traditional trails that have not succumbed to the widening axe.

Skiers of all levels will find something to make them happy here. Even the easy trails, which include the golf course and trails in the woods, offer beginners excellent valley views.

For intermediate and advanced skiers, we recommend a common loop, with an escape option for those hoping to avoid steep downhills. Take Pine Pass to Paradise Run, a narrow, twisting, uphill trail that is also fun to try in reverse. Ski all the way up Paradise Run to Moose Trail. Make a left on Moose Trail and continue up to Peter Grover Hill Loop. Ski to the intersection of Peter Grover and Hedgehog Highway. Decision time. Continuing on Peter Grover involves another 6–7 km of skiing, plus several challenging downhills. If you're growing weary or don't want to rise to the challenge, head back to the inn on Hedgehog. Otherwise, continue on Peter Grover, which eventually loops back to the inn.

The schematic trail map functions reasonably well, but it does not include the length of each trail.

Extras:

RACES: There are 5- and 10-km races. Call for information.

SPECIAL EVENTS: Waxing clinics, guided tours, and moonlight skiing.

OTHER: Sleigh rides, ice-skating, and full-sized sauna.

Travel Instructions:

FROM BOSTON: Take I-95 north to exit 11 and follow Route 26 north and west to Bethel.

FROM NEW YORK: From I-95 proceed as outlined above.

Although you cover a lot of highway on the way to Bethel, the drive is relatively safe as most of the roads are interstate highways, and Route 26 is usually well maintained.

The Birches

P.O. BOX 81
ROCKWOOD, MAINE 04478

For Ski Conditions:

HOURS OF OPERATION: 9:00 A.M. to dusk, daily

SNOW PHONE: 207/534-7305

Profile:

TRAILS: The Birches has 15 trails, totaling approximately 35 km, of which 30 km are groomed and track set as needed. Most of the trails are rolled wall-to-wall, with tracks set on the right side. Thus, skating is possible on most trails. In addition, skiers are invited to use the 200-mile, groomed snowmobile-trail system connected to the Birches. The groomed ski-trail system is classified as 51 percent easy, 26 percent more difficult, and 23 percent most difficult.

GROOMING: Average. The Birches does not use state-of-the-art grooming equipment. They do not possess a powder maker to groom during frozen conditions. Nevertheless, we have skied these trails on marginal days (other than frozen conditions) and found the system to be very skiable.

RENTALS: The Birches does not have an abundance of rental equipment. They have about 30 pairs of waxless skis (Rossignol and Karhu) and a few pairs of waxable skis, mounted with either SNS or 75-mm bindings, matched by Salomon boots and a variety of 75-mm boots. No racing skis are available, but they do rent snowshoes.

FOR WAX LOVERS: A complete supply of wax accessories is available. There is a heated waxing area in the basement of the main building.

FOOD & LODGING: You will never mistake this territory for suburban landscape. This ski center is definitely remote. The Birches consists of 17 hand-hewn cabins nestled in a grove of birch trees beside Moosehead Lake. The cabins are wood heated and supplied with cookstoves, utensils, and running water. No maid service is provided. Guests share a central shower and

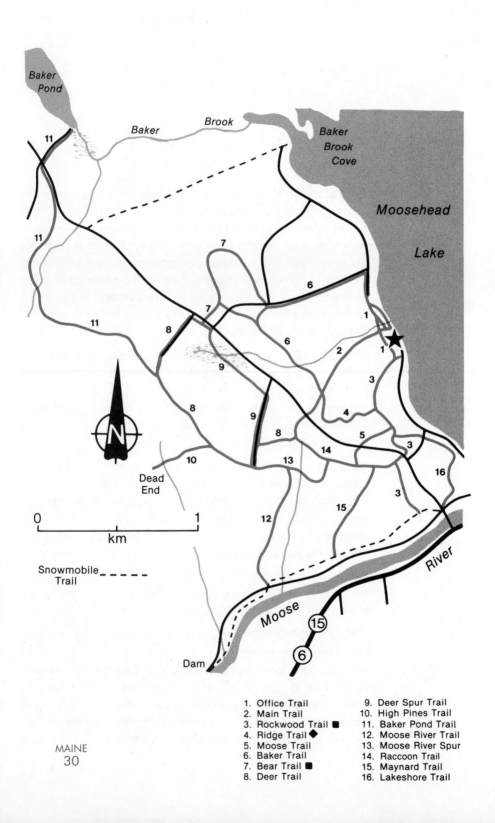

Baker
Pond

Baker   Brook

11

Baker
Brook
Cove

Moosehead

Lake

11

7

11

6

7

8

6   1

9   2   1

3

8   4

9   5

8   3

10   13   14

16

9

Dead
End

15

3

0   1

12

km

Snowmobile
Trail

River

Moose

15

6

Dam

1. Office Trail   9. Deer Spur Trail
2. Main Trail   10. High Pines Trail
3. Rockwood Trail ■   11. Baker Pond Trail
4. Ridge Trail ◆   12. Moose River Trail
5. Moose Trail   13. Moose River Spur
6. Baker Trail   14. Raccoon Trail
7. Bear Trail ■   15. Maynard Trail
8. Deer Trail   16. Lakeshore Trail

toilet facility, with (praise the Lord) hot water. There are other rooms available in the Rockwood area.

The ski center operates a restaurant that serves soups, sandwiches, hot entrees, and trail food. Other restaurants and watering holes can be found in nearby Rockwood, where the quantity and quality of the offerings is geared to the woodcutters and loggers who frequent these establishments.

ALPINE FACILITIES IN AREA: Squaw Mountain.

LESSONS: Instruction is available in traditional cross country skiing techniques. They do not teach skating or telemarking.

SAFETY: The trails are not patrolled during the day, nor are there end-of-the-day trail sweeps. They use a sign-in–sign-out monitoring system.

CHILDCARE FACILITIES: None.

Gestalt: Most of the trails at the Birches undulate across gently rolling timber stands. The lakeside trails afford spectacular views of Mount Kineo. Beginners can enjoy comfortable terrain and terrific vistas without having to engage in arduous ascents. Try a trip to Moose River on the easy trails: ski Main to Deer to Moose, then take the snowmobile trail across the bridge to Lakeshore, Rockwood, and Office back to base camp.

A solid day for intermediate skiers is a trip to Baker Pond and back on the Baker Pond Trail. Advanced skiers should attempt the ascent to the lookout tower atop Mount Kineo. Unfortunately, this trail is only skiable during better-than-average snow years.

For a fee, the cross country ski center will arrange inn-to-inn trips via old logging roads and wilderness trails or a backpacking adventure to Chimney Pond, an Alpine campsite surrounded by rock faces, icefalls, and snowfields. Reservations for these trips must be made well in advance.

The trail map needs a lot of improvement.

Extras: RACES: The Birches sponsors two 10-km and 3-km races each year, usually in January and March.

OTHER: The Birches also provides an outdoor hot tub and sauna for its guests.

Travel Instructions: FROM BOSTON: Take I-95 north to Newport, Maine. At Newport, take Route 7 north to Dover-Foxcroft. Pick up Route 15 west, which becomes Routes 15 and 6, and go through Greenville to Rockwood Strip. Cross the Moose River on a single-lane bridge and go two miles to the Birches.

FROM NEW YORK: From I-95 north proceed as outlined above.

All of the Maine roads are two-lane. The final two-mile stretch to the XC center is a dirt road. Call ahead for road conditions.

4

Carrabassett Valley
Ski Touring Center

CARRABASSETT VALLEY
KINGFIELD, MAINE 04947

**For Ski
Conditions:**

HOURS OF OPERATION: 9:00 A.M. to 5:00 P.M., daily. The lighted ice-skating rink is open until 8:00 P.M. on weekends and holidays.

SNOW PHONE: 207/237-2205
207/237-2000

Profile:

TRAILS: Carrabassett Valley has approximately 17 trails, totaling 85 km, although counting their trails is difficult because they think in terms of complete loops rather than connecting trails. They have 80 km of groomed and double-tracked trails. Despite the high quality and extra large size of this system, relatively few skiers find their way to central Maine, so skating is permitted on all trails until such time as the volume of skaters overwhelms the system. However, they prefer that you skate on the 7.5-km Competition Loop. The trail system is classified as 30 percent easy, 40 percent more difficult, and 30 percent most difficult.

GROOMING: Excellent. Carrabassett Valley uses state-of-the-art grooming equipment. Over the years they have improved the grading of the trails so that they can provide excellent skiing with only 8 to 12 inches of snow.

RENTALS: Carrabassett Valley rents Rossignol waxless skis with SNS bindings and Salomon boots. They do not rent waxable skis or racing skis, but they do have a few pairs of demonstration waxable skis. They also rent figure skates.

FOR WAX LOVERS: A complete supply of wax accessories is available. Waxing is allowed in a section of the woodstove-heated ski center, where a wax-encrusted picnic table serves as a waxing bench.

FOOD & LODGING: The cross country ski operation is housed in a soaring 3,800-square-foot passive-solar

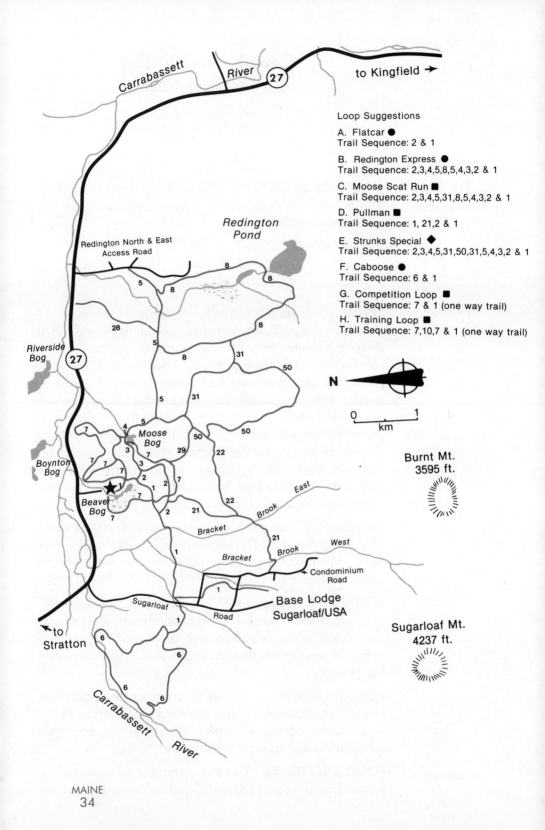

to Kingfield →

Carrabassett River

27

Redington Pond

Redington North & East Access Road

Riverside Bog

27

Moose Bog

Boynton Bog

Beaver Bog

East Brook

Bracket

Bracket Brook West

Condominium Road

Base Lodge Sugarloaf/USA

Sugarloaf Road

←to Stratton

Carrabassett River

Loop Suggestions

A. Flatcar ●
Trail Sequence: 2 & 1

B. Redington Express ●
Trail Sequence: 2,3,4,5,8,5,4,3,2 & 1

C. Moose Scat Run ■
Trail Sequence: 2,3,4,5,31,8,5,4,3,2 & 1

D. Pullman ■
Trail Sequence: 1, 21,2 & 1

E. Strunks Special ◆
Trail Sequence: 2,3,4,5,31,50,31,5,4,3,2 & 1

F. Caboose ●
Trail Sequence: 6 & 1

G. Competition Loop ■
Trail Sequence: 7 & 1 (one way trail)

H. Training Loop ■
Trail Sequence: 7,10,7 & 1 (one way trail)

N

0   1
km

Burnt Mt.
3595 ft.

Sugarloaf Mt.
4237 ft.

and multi-wood-stove-heated edifice. Typical skiers' fare (soup, chili, light lunches), prepared on a wood-fired cookstove, is offered in the large central section of the building, overlooking Sugarloaf Mountain, under the banner of the most unappetizing restaurant name we have ever heard: The Klister Kitchen. Yum, yum—please pass the red.

If you like the idea of skiing to your next meal, there are several other restaurants linked to the trail system: the Bag offers more of the same typical skiers' fare, Gepetto's serves pizza, and the Gladstone provides slightly more upscale nourishment.

More substantial food and comfort is provided by the Sugarloaf Inn, which is connected to the XC center by trail 1. The inn complex, which mainly services the Alpine area, offers hotel rooms and condominiums, and has recently added a superb sports facility featuring six whirlpool baths (both indoor and outdoor) to bubble away your aches and pains.

Many Nordic types prefer to avoid the Alpine crush and stay in nearby Kingfield where they can enjoy three of the best inns in New England: The Winter's Inn, a fully restored, mustard-colored, Victorian mansion overlooking the Carrabassett River; the Herbert, a 1917 hotel (built to impress the supporters of a local politician's bid for the state governorship) that features marble floors, unusual oak paneling, brass fixtures, and (for a touch of the modern) whirlpool-steambath units in many rooms; and Three Stanley Avenue, another splendid refurbished Victorian that is included in the National Historic Registry. Although each of these inns offers surprisingly sophisticated menus, we prefer the restaurant at Three Stanley Avenue (One Stanley Avenue)—continental cuisine with a New England twist—that one ski writer has dubbed "best in the state."

ALPINE FACILITIES IN AREA: Sugarloaf/USA, Saddleback.

LESSONS: Instruction is available in all methods of cross country skiing. However, management recommends learning telemarking and renting the appropriate equipment at the Sugarloaf Alpine facility.

SAFETY: Although the trails are not swept at the end of the day, they are patrolled during operating hours. Skiers are asked to register before embarking.

CHILDCARE FACILITIES: There is a day-care facility at the base lodge of Sugarloaf/USA.

Gestalt: Carrabassett Valley is the best cross country ski center in Maine and one of the top ten XC centers in New England. This trail system has everything we looked for in a great ski area: challenging terrain, intelligently cut trails, excellent grooming, beautiful vistas, and dedicated management.

Like the Jackson Ski Touring Center, Carrabassett Valley is owned by the town and managed by a non-profit community-development corporation formed by residents of the area. They have recently hired the Sugarloaf Corporation to oversee daily operations. As one acknowledgment of the civic responsibility of the XC center, the facility is made available to the five schools in the region. This partially explains how one of the best ski centers in New England can financially sustain itself, yet remain so relatively unknown and unskied by outsiders.

Be warned that for some of the trails, what is classified as "easiest" degree of difficulty would be considered "most difficult" at many other XC centers. For example, we would not hesitate to recommend that advanced and intermediate skiers try the 11.7-km trip to Redington Pond on the Redington Express Loop, even though the trail is classified as "easiest." The terrain on this loop is rolling, with a gradual climb up to Redington Pond, beautiful views of Bigelow Mountain, and an undulating cruise back to the center. If you want to add a little spice to the journey you can pick up the one-way Competition Loop on the return trip.

If you're seeking a little more downhill action, try the Pullman Loop (more difficult, 9 km) or the Strunks Special Loop (most difficult, 8.6 km). The Pullman Loop climbs to the base lodge at Sugarloaf/USA, where you can pause to get your fill of the Alpine scene and replenish carbohydrates for the screaming downhill return trip (which can be negotiated with a good snowplow). Strunks Special is a different story. It contains a

750-foot vertical drop that requires a lot of snow to be skiable, and you should not venture out on this loop if you don't have confidence in your technique.

For racers, the no-nonsense, 7.5-km Competition Loop is groomed for skating.

It is also worthwhile to note that Carrabassett Valley has one of the best maps and trail-marking systems in New England. The trail system is clearly displayed over a contour map of the area, and the outlines of eight recommended loops, with suggested trail sequence, are also presented.

Extras:

RACES: Carrabassett Valley hosts many races throughout the ski season. Call for additional information.

OTHER: The Sugartree Club at the Sugarloaf Inn, a complete sports facility open to the public, features an indoor pool, racquetball, saunas, steam room, hot tubs, Jacuzzis, and exercise equipment. And don't forget the aforementioned skating rink.

Travel Instructions:

FROM BOSTON: From I-95 north to Maine Turnpike, take exit 12 (Auburn) to Route 4. Follow Route 4 north through Farmington, to Route 27 north through Kingfield, to Carrabassett Valley Recreation Complex.

ALTERNATE ROUTE: In marginal weather conditions, some people prefer to take I-95 all the way up to Route 27 (near Augusta), then proceed as outlined above.

FROM NEW YORK: From I-95 proceed as outlined above.

Ski Nordic Touring Center
at Saddleback

P.O. BOX 490
RANGELEY, MAINE 04970

For Ski Conditions:

HOURS OF OPERATION: 9:00 A.M. to 4:00 P.M., daily

SNOW PHONE: 207/864-5671

Profile:

TRAILS: Saddleback has about 20 trails (depending on how you want to count them), of which approximately 35 km are groomed and track set as needed. Most of the trails are rolled wall-to-wall, with tracks set on the right side to allow for skating on the rest of the trail. In addition, a groomed snowmobile-trail system wide enough for skating is accessible from the Saddleback network. The groomed ski-trail system is classified as 21 percent easy, 57 percent more difficult, and 22 percent most difficult.

GROOMING: Above average. Saddleback does not use state-of-the-art grooming equipment. They do not possess a powder maker to groom during frozen conditions, but because of their high elevation they rarely have a problem with ice. Saddleback probably has the highest elevations of any major cross country ski area in New England. The base lodge is at 2,500 feet, and some of the trails are over 4,000 feet. Therefore, the snow at Saddleback tends to be drier than most areas. Nevertheless, we recommend that you call ahead if you suspect icy conditions. If your suspicions are allayed you are sure to be pleased with the quality of grooming under nonmarginal conditions. They always roll the full width of their wide trails, and lay a single set of tracks on the right, in the optimum skiing direction.

RENTALS: Saddleback rents Trak T-1200 waxless skis with the Trak/Look integrated boot/binding system and Trak T-6000 telemark skis with Trak telemark boots.

FOR WAX LOVERS: A complete supply of wax accessories is available. The Saddleback base lodge is an excellent example of an Alpine-Nordic shared facility

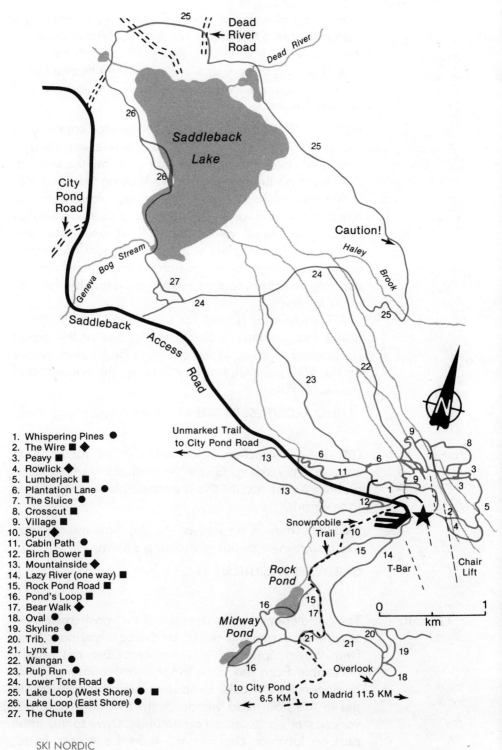

Dead River Road

Dead River

25

26

Saddleback Lake

City Pond Road

26

25

Caution!

Haley Brook

Geneva Bog Stream

27

24

24

25

Saddleback

Access Road

22

23

N

Unmarked Trail to City Pond Road

9

8

13

6

6

7

3

11

3

5

13

9

1

12

2

Snowmobile Trail

10

Rock Pond

15

14

1

T-Bar

Chair Lift

15

0   1

km

16

15

17

Midway Pond

16

21

21

21

20

19

Overlook

18

16

to City Pond 6.5 KM

to Madrid 11.5 KM

1. Whispering Pines ●
2. The Wire ■ ◆
3. Peavy ■
4. Rowlick ◆
5. Lumberjack ■
6. Plantation Lane ●
7. The Sluice ●
8. Crosscut ■
9. Village ■
10. Spur ◆
11. Cabin Path ●
12. Birch Bower ■
13. Mountainside ◆
14. Lazy River (one way) ■
15. Rock Pond Road ■
16. Pond's Loop ■
17. Bear Walk ◆
18. Oval ●
19. Skyline ●
20. Trib. ■
21. Lynx ■
22. Wangan ●
23. Pulp Run ●
24. Lower Tote Road ●
25. Lake Loop (West Shore) ● ■
26. Lake Loop (East Shore) ●
27. The Chute ■

that does not work very well. The Nordic operation is crammed into a tiny office, rendered almost invisible by the steady traffic of Alpine skiers. Although there is no official waxing station, one can wax in the heated basement of the base lodge, where there are lockers and electrical outlets.

FOOD & LODGING: There is a full-service cafeteria at the base lodge offering typical Alpine-skier-base-lodge fare. If you prefer to drink your lunch, climb the stairs to the tavern on the mezzanine overlooking the cafeteria.

The town of Rangeley is a recreation-related community that sports a variety of motels and rooming houses catering to skiers' needs, as well as one hotel, the Rangeley Inn, complete with entertainment and traditional Maine ambience. Condominiums from which you can step directly onto the ski trails are available for rent at Saddleback.

A favorite dining spot for traditional New England home style cooking is Doc Grant's, one of the oldest restaurants in town, which claims to be located exactly on the 45th parallel, halfway between the equator and the North Pole.

ALPINE FACILITIES IN AREA: Saddleback, Sugarloaf/ USA.

LESSONS: Instruction is available in all methods of cross country skiing. Given the availability of the Saddleback Alpine facility, this is a terrific place to learn how to telemark.

SAFETY: There is no end-of-the-day trail sweep. They use a sign-in–sign-out monitoring system.

CHILDCARE FACILITIES: Yes.

Gestalt: The Saddleback trail system is not the most convenient system for beginning skiers, as the best beginner trails (with the exception of a 1 km loop) are not readily accessible from the base lodge. We recommend that beginners try the Lake Loop; however, the only way to get to the trail head without first traversing more advanced trails is to use an automobile. Drive to the small parking lot near checkpoint 14 on the Access Road, park your car, and start skiing counterclockwise.

This trail system offers its best side (the mountain side) to intermediate and advanced skiers, who should enjoy the following loop: take Rock Pond Road to Rock Pond, continue on to Midway Pond, Midway Ridge, Lynx, and Bear Walk, to Overlook, Oval, and Skyline, where you will be rewarded with superb views of New Hampshire, Canada, and Vermont—on a clear day you can see over 100 miles. Return to the base lodge on Lazy River, a dreamy two-mile downhill run along gentle Alpine trails.

The trail map has been greatly improved, although they still do not present the length of each trail, which we consider an important safety feature.

Extras: RACES: Saddleback hosts several interscholastic races during the year.

SPECIAL EVENTS: Guided ski tours are available with advance notice: including 10-km Lake Loop Lunch Tours, featuring hot lunch served trailside, and night tours when the moon is full.

OTHER: The rental condominiums have access to hot tubs and saunas.

Travel Instructions: FROM BOSTON: Take I-95 north to Maine Turnpike exit 12 in Auburn. Pick up Route 4 and take it north to Rangeley. Follow the signs to Saddleback Mountain. Ski Nordic is located in the base lodge at the Alpine facility.

FROM NEW YORK: From I-95 north proceed as outlined above.

All of the Maine roads are two-lane and paved. There should be no travel hazards except during and immediately after snowstorms.

Sunday River
Cross Country Ski Center

R.F.D. 2, BOX 1688
BETHEL, MAINE 04217

For Ski Conditions:

HOURS OF OPERATION: 8:30 A.M. to 4:30 P.M., daily

SNOW PHONE: 207/824-2410

Profile:

TRAILS: Sunday River has 19 trails (though at least 10 of the trails closest to the inn are very short), totaling approximately 40 km, 32 km of which are groomed. They track set 20 km, and leave 8 km in their natural state. Skating is permitted on the 12 km of rolled trails, which include a 5-km race-training loop. The trail system is classified as 40 percent easy, 25 percent more difficult, and 35 percent most difficult.

GROOMING: Average. Sunday River does not have state-of-the-art grooming equipment, but they do a good job on most of the trail network. Due to equipment limitations they have trouble grooming the steeper sections during icy conditions.

RENTALS: Sunday River rents Fischer Crown waxless skis; a limited, mixed bag of waxable skis; and telemark skis. The touring skis are mounted with SNS bindings, matched by Salomon boots. They do not rent racing skis, but they do have a few pairs of snowshoes.

FOR WAX LOVERS: A complete supply of wax accessories is available. There is a heated waxing area with workbenches behind the ski center.

FOOD & LODGING: Bethel has a number of interesting inns, bed-and-breakfasts, and restaurants. The entire center of town has been designated a National Historic District.

The Sunday River Cross Country Ski Center was developed by the proprietors of the Sunday River Inn, which was originally built in 1965 to accommodate Alpine skiers from the nearby Sunday River ski area. The orientation of the inn is decidedly toward families on a

Covered
Bridge

Monkey Brook Road

19

N

0   1
km

21

20
18

19

Lean-to
17   18

13   16
15   9

12
9

11   10
13   14   8   7
12   9   5   6
13   1
3   2   4   2
1   4   1
1   22

Whitecap Lodge

1. Inn Loop ●   12. Tote Team ■
2. Bunny ●   13. Two Sled ■
3. Twitch ●   14. Sluice ■
4. Stone Wall ●   15. Pipeline ■
5. Fire Pit ●   16. Jill Poke ■
6. Ravine ●   17. Bateau ◆
7. Roll Away ●   18. Cruiser ◆
8. Gulch ●   19. Covered Bridge Trail ●
9. American Harrow ●   20. David's Drop ◆
10. Brown Jug ●   21. Overlook Trail ◆
11. Mystery ●   22. Locke Mountain Trail and Race Loop

budget. They specialize in adjusting living quarters to suit the size of your family, and in bring-your-own-sleeping-bag dorms.

Meals at the inn (baked ham, potatoes, and vegetables) are served at a family style buffet. Church groups, Boy Scout groups, families, etc., are the mainstay of their clientele, and not surprisingly, there is no bar on the premises. If you're a single skier seeking action, you can find all of the expected razzmatazz at the nearby Alpine facility. More sedate folk will find gentler options in the town of Bethel.

ALPINE FACILITIES IN AREA: Sunday River, Mount Abram.

LESSONS: Instruction is available in all methods of cross country skiing except skating. Take advantage of the adjacent Alpine facility and give telemarking a whirl.

SAFETY: There are no trail patrols during the day, nor trail sweeps at day's end. There is a sign-in–sign-out system.

CHILDCARE FACILITIES: None.

Gestalt:

Bethel boasts two enjoyable XC ski centers (Bethel Inn and Sunday River, combined trail system of 70 km) and surely demands consideration as one of the better ski towns in New England.

Many trail systems reflect the personalities of the ski center proprietors, so it is no surprise that the emphasis at Sunday River is on trails that the whole family can ski. The overwhelming favorite in this regard is the Covered Bridge Trail, a gently rolling novices' trek that passes through woods on the edge of a historic flood plain on the way to a covered bridge. Racers also find this trail a good training run and can return to the inn with a more challenging ascent up David's Drop and a long gradual descent down Two Sled.

Skiing in "reverse," the big thrill at Sunday River, is negotiating the 400-foot descent on David's Drop. One ski writer said, "it's like bobsledding on skis when there's no powder covering the trail."

The schematic trail map functions reasonably well, although it does not include the length of each trail.

Extras:

RACES: Sunday River usually hosts two or three citizens' races each year, one of which is part of the Maine Nordic Ski Council Series.

SPECIAL EVENTS: Every Friday night the center sponsors a kerosene-lamp-lighted ski to a bonfire, where the participants can gather and do traditional bonfire things (sing, roast marshmallows, etc.).

OTHER: The Sunday River Inn has a wood-fired sauna that the proprietors will ignite when the moment feels right.

Travel Instructions:

FROM BOSTON: Take I-95 north to exit 11, then Maine Route 26 northwest to Bethel. Sunday River is located three miles north of Bethel on Route 2 east—just follow the signs.

FROM NEW YORK: From I-95 proceed as outlined above.

7

Troll Valley Ski Touring Center

R.F.D. 4, BOX 5215
FARMINGTON, MAINE 04938

For Ski Conditions:

HOURS OF OPERATION: 9:00 A.M. to dusk, daily

SNOW PHONE: 207/778-3656
207/778-2830

Profile:

TRAILS: Troll Valley is the centerpiece of two trail networks connected by a common courtesy arrangement: Titcomb Mountain Ski Touring Center and Troll Valley. The combined system has about 15 trails (depending on how you want to count them), of which approximately 40 km are groomed and track set as needed. Most of the trails are rolled wall-to-wall, with tracks set on the right side to allow for skating on the rest of the trail. The Titcomb Mountain network was established as a racing system, and is frequently groomed for skating only.

In addition, a more-than-you-could-ever-ski, groomed snowmobile-trail system—also wide enough for skating—is accessible from Troll Valley. The groomed ski trails are classified as 64 percent easy, 24 percent more difficult, and 12 percent most difficult.

GROOMING: Above average. Troll Valley and Titcomb use state-of-the-art grooming equipment, though they lack a power tiller to groom during frozen conditions. They do possess a powder maker, however. Nevertheless, we recommend that you call ahead if you suspect icy conditions. They always roll the full width of their trails and lay a single set of tracks on the right side— always in the optimum skiing direction.

RENTALS: A very limited supply of rental equipment is available: Karhu waxless skis, a variety of waxable skis, with a mélange of Salomon, Trak, and Adidas boots and bindings. They also have four pairs of racing skis and two pairs of snowshoes. If you need to rent equipment, we recommend you make reservations.

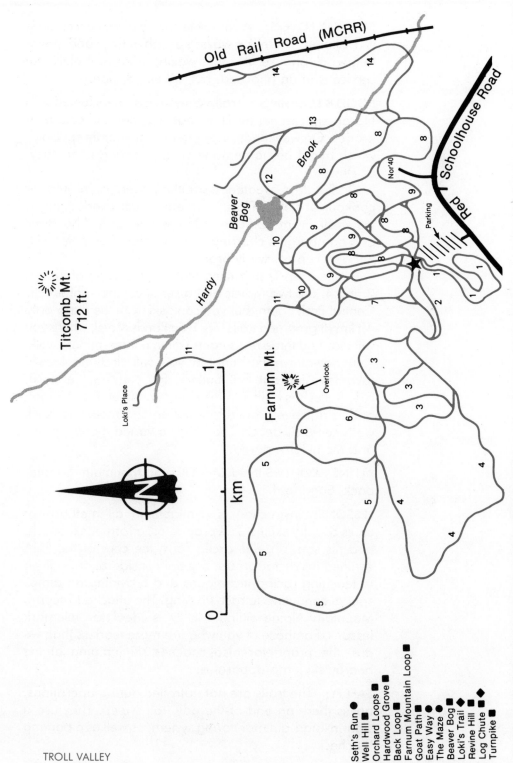

Titcomb Mt.
712 ft.

Old Rail Road (MCRR)

Schoolhouse Road

Rep

Beaver Bog

Brook

Hardy

Loki's Place

Parking

Nor'40

Farnum Mt.

Overlook

N

km
0   1

1. Seth's Run ●
2. Well Hill ■
3. Orchard Loops ■
4. Hardwood Grove ■
5. Back Loop ■
6. Farnum Mountain Loop ■
7. Goat Path ■
8. Easy Way ●
9. The Maze ●
10. Beaver Bog ■
11. Loki's Trail ◆
12. Revine Hill ◆
13. Log Chute ◆
14. Turnpike ■

FOR WAX LOVERS: A complete supply of wax accessories is available. There is a waxing bench in the wood-stove-heated clubhouse. Another waxing area with electrical service is in an attached, but unheated, garage.

FOOD & LODGING: Troll Valley keeps skiers fueled with Nordic snacks: sandwiches, pastries, hot and cold beverages. On weekends, they offer a "blue plate special," which might be homemade chili, chowder, chop suey, or stew.

On Sundays, weather permitting, there is an outdoor cookout at Loki's Place, a scenic knoll overlooking a waterfall. From 12:00 to 2:00 P.M. the sizzle of hot dogs and hamburgers charring over hot coals competes with the gurgling of Hardy Brook.

A mile from Troll Valley, at the intersection of Routes 2 and 4, are two motels and a set of cabins—not exactly Central Park South, but you can't ski from the Plaza onto 40 km of groomed trails. Try Twin Ponds Motel, where you will also find three restaurants within a three-minute walk.

In downtown Farmington you will find the locals' favorite restaurant, F. L. Butler's. Formerly a warehouse, F. L. Butler's is built into the side of a hill on Front Street, and its massive granite foundation and repointed brick walls serve as decor. They offer a varied menu, spirits, and Maine-size portions.

ALPINE FACILITIES IN AREA: Titcomb Mountain, Saddleback, Sugarloaf/USA.

LESSONS: Instruction is available in all methods of cross country skiing. The proprietor, a former ski coach, and his son, an elite racer, form the core of the PSIA certified instructor group. Special consideration is given to teaching racing techniques and providing an atmosphere conducive to race training. The attached Titcomb Mountain Alpine skiing facility is ideal for telemark lessons. For those of you who are more fearless than we are, the proprietor also coaches ski jumping at the nearby ski jump apparatus.

SAFETY: The trails are not patrolled during operations, nor is there an end-of-the-day trail sweep. They use a sign-in–sign-out monitoring system, as well as a parking lot check.

CHILDCARE FACILITIES: None.

Gestalt: All of the trails in this network were designed and built under the direction of the proprietor—many during his days of coaching and prior to his management of the Troll Valley operation.

From the clubhouse, a short, gradual downhill trail leads to the flats of the Nor' 40 Campground section of the system, where there are primarily easy trails for beginners. Those seeking the racecourse at the Titcomb complex must pass through the Nor' 40 area first. In the opposite direction from the clubhouse, a gentle, 200-meter ascent leads to the intermediate trails in the scenic orchard area and beyond to Farnum Mountain, where the difficulty of the skiing increases.

Not surprisingly, each system tends to be favored by the level of skier for which it was designed. For beginners we recommend Nor' 40 and Loki's "hamburger haven"; intermediates, the orchard loops and parts of Farnum Mountain; experts, Titcomb raceway and the more challenging trails on Farnum.

The trail map needs a lot of improvement.

Extras: RACES: Loki's Loppet, a race in the Maine Nordic Council Series.

SPECIAL EVENTS: Guided ski trips and moonlight tours are available with advance notice.

OTHER: A complete fitness center is located at the cross country ski area.

Travel Instructions: FROM BOSTON: Take I-95 north to Maine Turnpike to exit 12 in Auburn, Maine. Pick up Route 4 and take it all the way to Wilton. Seven miles past Wilton, just beyond a shopping center, turn left at the Red School House; touring center is one more mile.

FROM NEW YORK: Take I-95 north. Proceed as outlined above.

All of the Maine roads are two-lane and paved. There should be no travel hazards except during and immediately after snowstorms.

Massachusetts

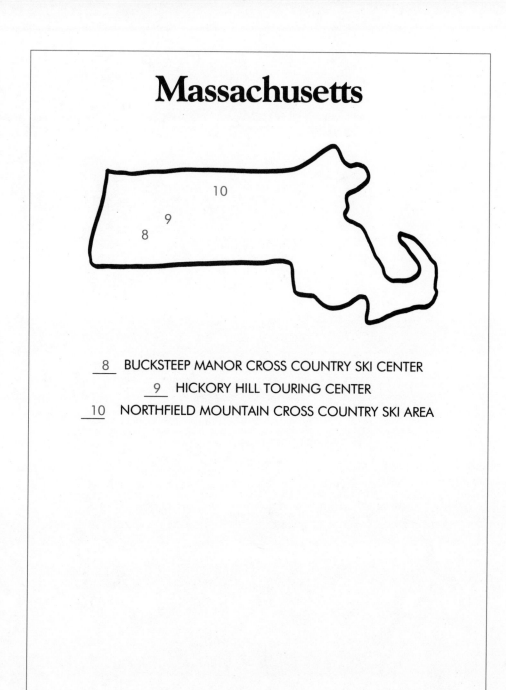

__8__ BUCKSTEEP MANOR CROSS COUNTRY SKI CENTER

__9__ HICKORY HILL TOURING CENTER

__10__ NORTHFIELD MOUNTAIN CROSS COUNTRY SKI AREA

Bucksteep Manor
Cross Country Ski Center

WASHINGTON MOUNTAIN ROAD
WASHINGTON, MASSACHUSETTS 01223

For Ski Conditions:

HOURS OF OPERATION: 8:00 A.M. to 4:30 P.M., daily

SNOW PHONE: 413/623-6651
413/623-5535 (inn)

Profile:

TRAILS: Bucksteep has 16 trails, totaling approximately 20 km, all of which are groomed and track set as needed. None of the trails is groomed specifically for skating. The trail system is classified as 50 percent easy, 25 percent more difficult, and 25 percent most difficult.

GROOMING: Average. Bucksteep's grooming equipment is not state of the art. Although they do possess a powder maker for breaking up frozen snow, we recommend that you call ahead if you suspect icy conditions.

RENTALS: Bucksteep rents Rossignol waxless skis and a few pairs of Rossignol waxable skis, all of which are mounted with Salomon (SNS) bindings and matching Salomon boots. They also rent racing skis.

FOR WAX LOVERS: A complete selection of wax accessories is available. Skiers wax at one of three well-built workbenches with braces in the wood-stove-heated ski shop.

FOOD & LODGING: Bucksteep Manor was built at the turn of the century mimicking the design of an estate in England. Today, it feels like a down-home, natural foods sort of place that exudes warmth and friendliness.

The inn offers simple, spacious rooms and, for rustic souls, several wood-stove-heated cabins devoid of modern utilities.

At the Manor Kitchen hearty, homemade natural foods are served in a lodge-like atmosphere. The menu changes regularly.

In addition, the old carriage barn has been converted into a small, truly funky bar that opens up into a large

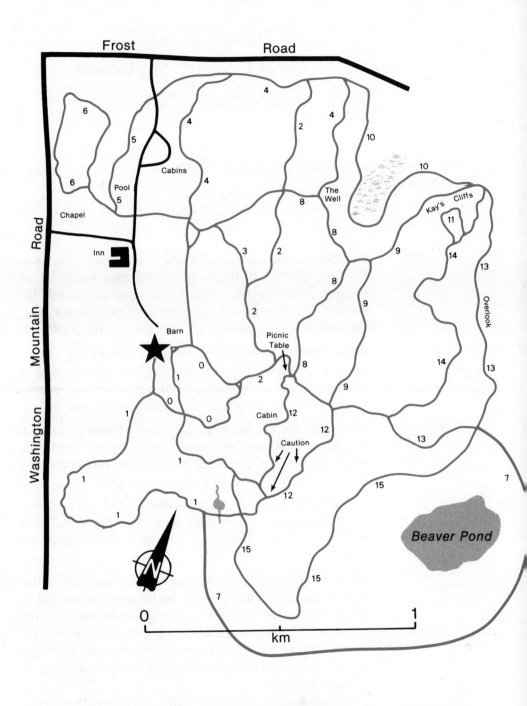

Frost Road

6
5
6
Pool 5
Cabins
Chapel
Road
Inn
Washington Mountain Road
Barn
★

4
4
4
4
2
10
10
The Well
Kay's Cliffs
11
14
13
Overlook
3
2
8
8
9
2
8
9
13
Picnic Table
8
14
2
Cabin
12
9
13
0
1
0
0
Caution
12
12
1
13
7
1
12
15
1
15
Beaver Pond
7
15
15
7

N

0   1
km

0. Over Easy ●
1. Pine Run ●
2. Strider ●
3. Stage Trail ●
4. Well Run ●
5. Karu Trail ●
6. Chapel Loop ●
7. Randy's Way ●
8. Creo Trail ■
9. Deer Run ■
10. Fannelli's Glade ■
11. Cliff Walk ■
12. Mad Dog Loop ◆
13. Ridge Run ◆
14. Rudy's Spur ◆
15. Mu's Mile ◆

dance spot on weekends, where live bands keep the joint jumpin'.

ALPINE FACILITIES IN AREA: Brodie Mountain, Jiminy Peak, Otis Ridge, Butternut Basin.

LESSONS: Instruction is available in traditional cross country skiing techniques.

SAFETY: The trails are patrolled during the day, but there are no trail sweeps at the end of the day.

CHILDCARE FACILITIES: None.

Gestalt:

We have included Bucksteep Manor in our guide because there are only a handful of good cross country ski areas in Massachusetts (where Bucksteep ranks in the top five), and because of its proximity to New York (only 150 miles from New York City).

Intermediate skiers can easily handle all of the trails; however, skiers of all skill levels can have a good time at Bucksteep.

An enjoyable loop for advanced beginners and more experienced skiers is the following: from the ski shop head out on Well Run to Creo Trail, Deer Run, and Ridge Run to Mad Dog Loop, and then Pine Run back to the ski shop.

Bucksteep offers a good trail map that clearly indicates the location of downhill runs. However, the map does not include the distance of each trail, which we consider an important safety feature.

Extras:

RACES: Bucksteep usually sponsors several races each year, including the Bucksteep Citizen's Race, the Berkshire Masters Championship, and the Bill Koch Youth Ski League races.

SPECIAL EVENTS: Sleigh rides, full moon tours, and other guided tours.

Travel Instructions:

FROM BOSTON: Take I-90 west (Massachusetts Turnpike) to exit 2 (Lee). Take Route 20 east four miles to Becket Road, go left on Becket Road, and travel four miles to a stop sign (McNerney Road). Go left on McNerney; touring center is four miles on the right. It takes 15–20 minutes to go from the I-90 exit to Bucksteep Manor.

FROM NEW YORK: Follow the Taconic State Parkway to I-90 east; in Massachusetts get off at exit 2 and proceed as outlined above.

The roads are generally well maintained.

Hickory Hill Touring Center

BUFFINGTON HILL ROAD
WORTHINGTON, MASSACHUSETTS 01098

For Ski Conditions:

HOURS OF OPERATION: 9:00 A.M. to 5:00 P.M., daily

SNOW PHONE: 413/238-5813 (24 hours)

Profile:

TRAILS: Hickory Hill has 25 trails, totaling approximately 35 km, all of which are groomed and track set as often as twice a day if necessary. All of the trails are 15 to 17 feet wide to accommodate skating. The trail system is classified as 20 percent easy, 46 percent more difficult, and 34 percent most difficult.

GROOMING: Excellent. Hickory Hill uses state-of-the-art grooming equipment. We skied this system on a marginal day when a well-known nearby XC center was icy and dangerous, and found the Hickory Hill trails to be in superb condition.

RENTALS: Hickory Hill rents Rossignol waxless skis and a variety of Atomic waxable skis, all with Salomon (SNS) bindings and matching Salomon boots. They also have several pairs of Rossignol racing skis.

FOR WAX LOVERS: A complete supply of wax accessories is available. Waxing is permitted in the ski shop and the recreation barn (for want of a better term), both of which are heated.

FOOD & LODGING: Adjacent to the ski shop is a large barn, heated by a fireplace, that houses a snack bar offering hot soups, sandwiches, coffee, cookies, etc., and a spirits bar.

The cross country ski center is located on the Lafayette Trail in the Berkshire hill town of Worthington, where there are several bed-and-breakfast inns, but not the clutter of hastily built condos and motels that abound in many ski towns. One of the favorite bed and breakfasts is the Worthington Inn at Four Corners Farm.

If you need a variety of restaurants to choose from at the end of the day, the best bet is to drive to the college town

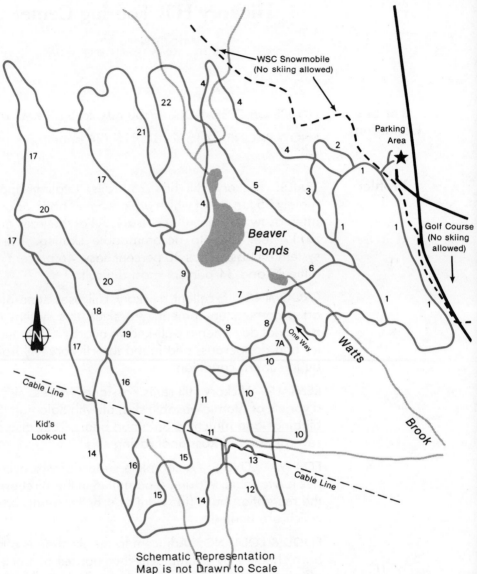

WSC Snowmobile
(No skiing allowed)

Parking
Area

Golf Course
(No skiing allowed)

Beaver
Ponds

Watts

Brook

One Way

7A

Cable Line

Kid's
Look-out

Cable Line

N

Schematic Representation
Map is not Drawn to Scale

1. The Big Field ●
2. Coy Dog ●
3. Weasel Hill ■
4. Dog's Leg ■
5. Ringtail Run ●
6. Trout Bridge ■
7. Fiddlehead ■
7A. Crab Apple ●
8. Quill Run ●
9. Fox Path ■
10. Parson Lot ●
11. Stone Walls ◆

12. Pine Hawk ■
13. Tailors Connection ■
14. Twin Springs ■
15. Blue Stone Hollow ■
16. Bucks Crossing ■
17. Cat's Paw ■
18. Tree Den ■
19. Bear Hill ◆
20. Yellow Birch Trail ■
21. Jack Rabbit ◆
22. Snow Goose ■

of Northampton (15 miles, on the way to Boston), where everything from college food to nouvelle cuisine is available.

ALPINE FACILITIES IN AREA: Brodie Mountain, Berkshire Snow Basin, Blandford, Berkshire East.

LESSONS: Instruction is available in all methods of cross country skiing.

SAFETY: On weekends the trails are patrolled by at least one member of the Berkshire Nordic Ski Patrol, but there are no end-of-the-day trail sweeps. Management's penchant for constant grooming enhances safety, as the grooming machine is equipped with a two-way radio. Management also monitors cars left in the parking lot at the end of the day.

CHILDCARE FACILITIES: None.

Gestalt: The Hickory Hill Touring Center may be the best kept secret in New England Nordic skiing. Their trails and grooming are comparable to the best XC centers in the East, but no one we spoke with while compiling information for this book had ever heard of the place.

The good news for skiers in Connecticut and New York is that Hickory Hill is only 3½ hours from New York City. The bad news is that this Berkshire location also means that spotty snow cover is possible, so definitely call ahead for snow conditions.

The perimeter loop is a fun ski for intermediate and advanced skiers. From the XC center, ski across The Big Field to Trout Bridge to Quill Run, which bisects Parson Lot and leads to Pine Hawk. Pine Hawk is the beginning of a less than arduous ascent that includes Twin Springs and the first half of Cat's Paw. Cat's Paw crests at a modest scenic vista, where some like to break for a picnic. The rest of Cat's Paw is a rollicking descent, but you should stop and turn left onto Crooked Leg Hill (a trail added to the system for the 1986–87 season, not shown on map), which is the best downhill run in the network. Ski back up to the center via Dog's Leg or Ringtail Run.

Hickory Hill offers a legible, accurate, contoured trail map. The map's only defect is that it does not include the distance of each trail, which we consider to be important information.

Extras:

RACES: None.

SPECIAL EVENTS: Full moon ski parties.

OTHER: While the sedate town of Worthington tries to keep a lid on sensory pleasures, those still in need of stimulus after a hard day of skiing can drive to Northampton, which services the many colleges in the area.

Travel Instructions:

FROM BOSTON: The Town of Worthington frowns on signs. As a consequence of country charm conceit, on our first visit we passed through Worthington three times before we found the XC center. There are several ways to get to Worthington, but only one way we recommend.

Take I-90 west (Massachusetts Turnpike) to exit 3, Westfield. From the turnpike tollbooth, turn right onto routes 202 and 10 south. At the fifth traffic light, turn right onto Route 20 west to Huntington, where you take Route 112 north to the center of Worthington. There is only one traffic light in the center of Worthington; make a left at the light onto Buffington Hill Road, which goes straight to Hickory Hill.

FROM NEW YORK: Take I-91 north to Springfield and pick up Route 20 west. Take Route 20 west to Huntington and proceed as outlined above.

Route 112 can be treacherous in foul weather; call ahead for road conditions.

Northfield Mountain
Cross Country Ski Area

P.O. BOX 377 R.R. 1
NORTHFIELD, MASSACHUSETTS 01360

For Ski Conditions:

HOURS OF OPERATION: 9:00 A.M. to 5:00 P.M., daily

SNOW PHONE: 413/659-3713
413/659-3714

Profile:

TRAILS: Northfield has 16 trails, totaling approximately 40 km, all of which are groomed and double-track set where appropriate. All of the "most difficult" trails have been groomed for both skating and diagonal stride. Skating is also permitted on any other trails where skating would not ruin the set tracks. The trail system is classified as 30 percent easy, 50 percent more difficult, and 20 percent most difficult.

GROOMING: Excellent. Northfield uses state-of-the-art grooming equipment. Conditions permitting, all trails are groomed daily from 1:00 A.M. to 9:00 A.M. Northfield also offers the most meticulously prepared trails in New England. After the trails were initially cut and graded they were covered with wood chips to retard plant growth and to enhance trail maintenance.

RENTALS: A huge selection of rental equipment is available: Fischer, Trak, and Rossignol waxless skis, Salomon boots to match SNS bindings, and 40 pairs of snowshoes. Skate skis and poles are also available.

FOR WAX LOVERS: A complete supply of wax accessories is available. Beside the ski shop is an unheated waxing room with workbenches.

FOOD & LODGING: On weekends and holidays the XC center features an outdoor barbecue and grill that is the perfect repast after a bit of skiing. Besides offering the standard charcoaled fare of hot dogs and hamburgers, the grill caters to the dietary demands of nonmeat eaters by providing "hamburgers" made out of tofu. Don't knock it till you've tried it—besides, everything tastes

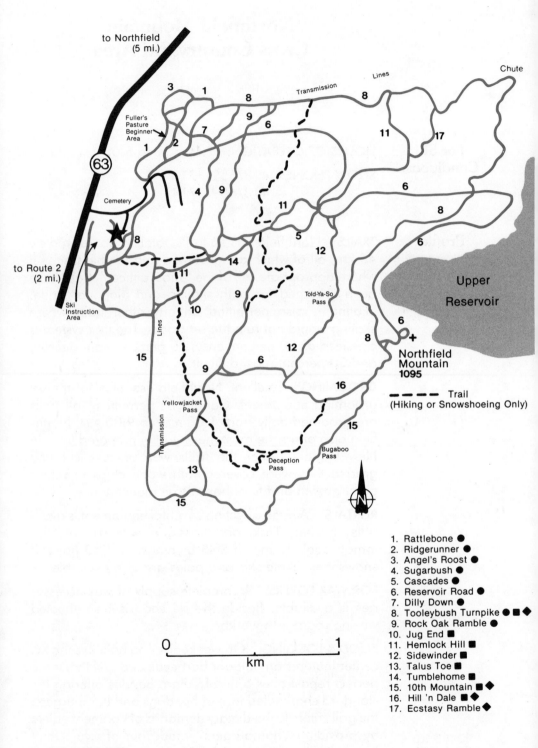

to Northfield
(5 mi.)

Chute

Lines

Transmission

3   1   8   8

Fuller's
Pasture
Beginner
Area

9

7   6   11   17

1

(63)   2

Cemetery   6

4   9   8

8

11

to Route 2
(2 mi.)

5

Ski
Instruction
Area

14

11   12

Upper

Reservoir

10

Told-Ya-So
Pass

6

8

9   6

Lines

15   8   Northfield
Mountain
1095

Transmission

9   6   12

Yellowjacket
Pass   16   15

Trail
(Hiking or Snowshoeing Only)

13   Deception
Pass   Bugaboo
Pass

15

N

0   1

km

1. Rattlebone ●
2. Ridgerunner ●
3. Angel's Roost ●
4. Sugarbush ●
5. Cascades ●
6. Reservoir Road ●
7. Dilly Down ●
8. Tooleybush Turnpike ● ■ ◆
9. Rock Oak Ramble ●
10. Jug End ■
11. Hemlock Hill ■
12. Sidewinder ■
13. Talus Toe ■
14. Tumblehome ■
15. 10th Mountain ■ ◆
16. Hill 'n Dale ■ ◆
17. Ecstasy Ramble ◆

great after a hard ski on a cold, crisp day. Midway up the mountain, in a spot attainable by all levels of skiers, is the Chocolate Pot—a cute shed where hot cocoa and lemonade are dispensed on weekends and holidays.

Lodging and restaurants are available in the nearby town of Northfield. The Northfield County House, a bed and breakfast, is a local favorite, as is Phases, a mountaintop restaurant with spectacular views and reasonable prices.

ALPINE FACILITIES IN AREA: None.

LESSONS: Instruction is available in all methods of cross country skiing. Northfield rightfully prides itself on the quality and quantity of its instructors. They also provide an excellent instruction and practice area, where you are likely to encounter hundreds of skiers making sitzmarks for the first time.

SAFETY: Northfield boasts the most comprehensive Nordic patrol system in New England. They have an official NSP Nordic Ski Patrol program, manned by over 20 volunteers and 3 full-time staffers. All ski patrol members receive the equivalent of a week's worth of training. It seemed as if every time we consulted our trail map we were approached by a helpful ski patroller. The ski patrol is supported by an emergency medical facility at the ski lodge. All trails are swept at the end of the day. In addition, Northfield's unusually wide trails help prevent novice skiers from mating with tree trunks.

CHILDCARE FACILITIES: None.

Gestalt: To paraphrase an appellation applied to George Steinbrenner's New York Yankees, Northfield is the best cross country ski area money can buy. The Northfield Mountain Cross Country Ski Area was conceived and financed by a utility company. One-half mile beneath the mountain's surface lies a giant pumped-storage hydroelectric station—which also explains the huge reservoir on top of the mountain. This may all appear too James Bondish for some, but the net result is an outstanding ski facility, dedicated to constantly improving the average citizen's ability to enjoy this sport, where finances rarely stand in the way of the needs of the cross country ski area.

Unfortunately, like the Yankees, Northfield is discovering that utopia cannot always be purchased. In the past few years the Northfield area has been plagued by that dread disease, "lack-a-snow." In one particularly bad year they were open for only six days of skiing.

When Northfield is experiencing a good snow season, the quality of the trail system combined with its proximity to major metropolitan areas make it a natural magnet for many skiers. As a result, Northfield can get overcrowded, so we recommend that you ask about crowds when you call for snow conditions. However, you should not be deterred from skiing these excellent tracks by visions of people-packed trails; instead, sacrifice a few hours of sleep and arrive early.

Advanced skiers should try the perimeter loop, Tooleybush Turnpike and 10th Mountain, which offers several vistas along its 11.7 km.

Intermediate skiers may enjoy the following route: take Tooleybush to Hemlock Hill, go up Hemlock Hill to Sidewinder, continue on upper Hill 'N Dale to 10th Mountain. Make a left on 10th Mountain and reconnect with Tooleybush. Ski Tooleybush to marker R3 and return to the lodge via Reservoir Road.

Extras:
RACES: AM/KM on the Sunday before Valentine's Day; start time is 8:00 A.M.

SPECIAL EVENTS: Northfield sponsors waxing clinics, seminars, guided tours, and night ski tours.

OTHER: In nearby Greenfield are two spas with saunas and hot tubs.

Travel Instructions:
FROM BOSTON: Take Route 2 west to Route 63 (near Erving). Head north on Route 63 2½ miles to touring center.

FROM NEW YORK: I-91 north to exit 27 (Route 2 east). Take Route 2 east for about eight miles to the intersection of Route 63. Proceed as outlined above.

These roads are usually well maintained.

New Hampshire

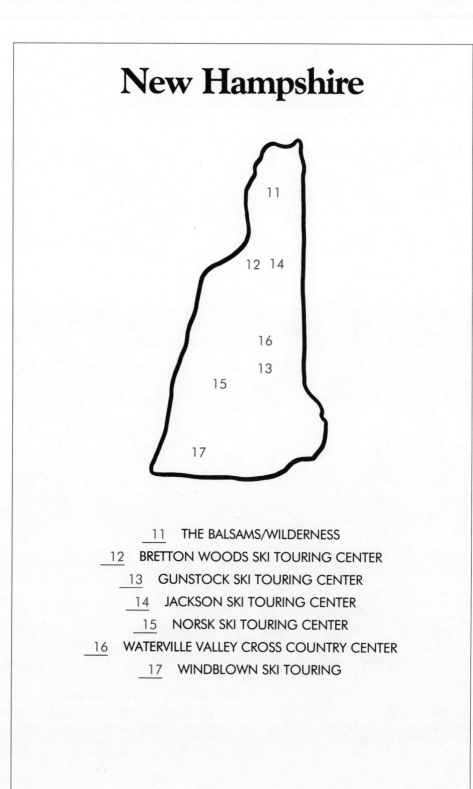

11   THE BALSAMS/WILDERNESS

12   BRETTON WOODS SKI TOURING CENTER

13   GUNSTOCK SKI TOURING CENTER

14   JACKSON SKI TOURING CENTER

15   NORSK SKI TOURING CENTER

16   WATERVILLE VALLEY CROSS COUNTRY CENTER

17   WINDBLOWN SKI TOURING

The Balsams/Wilderness

DIXVILLE NOTCH, NEW HAMPSHIRE 03576

For Ski Conditions:

HOURS OF OPERATION: 9:00 A.M. to 4:00 P.M., daily

SNOW PHONE: 800/255-0600 (Continental United States)

800/255-0800 (New Hampshire)

603/255-3400 (direct dial)

603/255-3951 (base lodge)

Profile:

TRAILS: The Balsams has 20 trails. Approximately 45 km are groomed and track set daily. Most of the trails have been widened to accommodate both skating and classic skiing. All of the trails may be skied in two directions. The trail system is classified as 18 percent easy, 70 percent more difficult, and 12 percent most difficult.

GROOMING: Excellent. The Balsams has a fleet of top-quality grooming equipment and the ability to groom in icy conditions.

RENTALS: Trak is the name of the rental equipment here: waxless skis, boots, bindings, and poles. Other brand names may be found on waxable skis and a few pairs of demonstration racing skis. They also rent snowshoes.

FOR WAX LOVERS: A complete supply of wax accessories is available. The Balsams has a very civilized waxing facility. There is abundant heat to keep tootsies toasty and waxes soft, as well as a waxing table with ski braces.

FOOD & LODGING: The Balsams calls itself "The Switzerland of America," a title bestowed on the area by nineteenth-century guidebook writers. The hotel does rise elegantly out of Dixville Notch and from the outside bears a resemblance to more legendary resorts such as Saint-Moritz. Inside, management has initiated a tasteful renovation policy, upgrading five to seven bedrooms each year during mud season—request a renovated room. If you can afford $390 to $450 per night, the Tower Suite, a multi-level extravaganza with a large

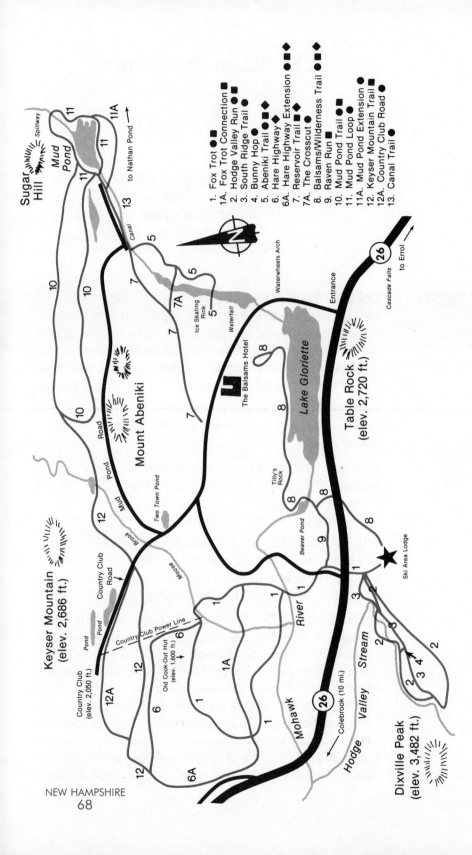

Sugar Hill
Spillway
Mud Pond
11
11
11A
11
11
13
to Nathan Pond
Canal
5
7
5
5
7A
Ice Skating Rink
5
Waterfall
7
Mount Abeniki
7
The Balsams Hotel
8
8
Lake Gloriette
Waterwheels Arch
Table Rock
(elev. 2,720 ft.)
Entrance
26
to Errol
Cascade Falls
8
Tilly's Rock
8
8
8
Beaver Pond
9
8
Two Town Pond
★
Ski Area Lodge
1
Keyser Mountain
(elev. 2,686 ft.)
10
10
Road
10
Mud
12
Pond
Brook
Country Club Road
Moose
Country Club Power Line
Pond
Old Cook-Out Hut
(elev. 1,600 ft.)
6
1
12
1A
1
1
River
Country Club
(elev. 2,050 ft.)
12A
12
6
1
Mohawk
26
Colebrook (10 mi.)
Hodge Valley Stream
3
2
3
8
2
3
4
2
2
Dixville Peak
(elev. 3,482 ft.)
12
6A

N

1. Fox Trot ●■
1A. Fox Trot Connection ■
2. Hodge Valley Run ●
3. South Ridge Trail ●
4. Bunny Hop ●
5. Abeniki Trail ◆
6. Hare Highway ◆
6A. Hare Highway Extension ●
7. Reservoir Trail ◆
7A. The Crosscut ■
8. Balsams/Wilderness Trail ■
9. Raven Run ●
10. Mud Pond Trail ●
11. Mud Pond Loop ●
11A. Mud Pond Extension ■
12. Keyser Mountain Trail ●
12A. Country Club Road ●
13. Canal Trail ●

NEW HAMPSHIRE
68

Jacuzzi and a 360-degree view from the tower bedroom, is a must. It is difficult to get a reservation, as satisfied clientele return year after year, so it is essential to make reservations early.

The hotel also prides itself on its food. It is abundant. And the breakfasts are as good as they come. Soups and other fast foods are available in the base lodge at the ski area, which services both Alpine and Nordic skiers.

Although food and lodging are available in the town of Colebrook, the Balsams is a self-contained destination resort, and a first-time visitor to the area should experience everything the hotel has to offer before inquiring about other possibilities.

ALPINE FACILITIES IN AREA: Wilderness, the mountain owned and operated by the Balsams for its guests.

LESSONS: Instruction is available in all methods of cross country skiing. Since both Alpine and Nordic activities are coordinated from the same building, this is a good place to learn telemarking.

For a modest fee, the instructors will arrange for a video-taped ski lesson and review your ski form in slow motion, over cocktails, in the evening.

SAFETY: There are no regular patrols or end-of-the-day trail sweeps, but everyone is required to register at the ski-school desk at the base lodge before embarking on the trails.

CHILDCARE FACILITIES: Yes.

Gestalt:

The Balsams/Wilderness is one of the most unusual ski areas in New England. To begin with, it is rare to find Alpine and Nordic skiers comfortably sharing the same base lodge and embarking from the same location without a sense of overcrowding. This is mainly due to the remoteness of the Balsams and the fact that 95 percent of the skiers are guests of the hotel. It is also extraordinarily beautiful; in fact, one could easily argue that this is the most beautiful of New England's ski areas, as Dixville Notch is truly breathtaking.

If you are an inexperienced skier, we recommend that you take the shuttle bus from the hotel to the base lodge and test your skills on the easiest trails in that area before trying the more remote trails that begin at the hotel.

For intermediate and advanced skiers, we recommend the following loops for successive days: on the first day take the Balsams Wilderness Trail from the hotel to the base lodge. Stop to talk to a ski instructor and explore what the area has to offer. Then take Fox Trot to Hare Highway and make the 2-km loop back to Fox Trot. Continue on Fox Trot to Raven Run, which intersects homeward-bound Balsams/Wilderness Trail. On the second day head in the opposite direction. Cross the parking lot behind the hotel and walk over to the skating rink where Abeniki Trail begins. Ski up Abeniki to Reservoir Trail. An accounting is required at this intersection: if you're still full of energy, ski across the flat and boring Canal Trail (a wide road shared by snowmobilers) to Mud Pond Loop and Mud Pond Trail. If the large Balsam breakfasts are slowing you down, you should seriously consider returning to the hotel on Reservoir Trail, which is a fun downhill run.

The new Balsams' trail map couldn't be better. It's printed on coated paper and features an artist's rendering of the terrain; length, degree of difficulty, and description of each trail; and even a kilometer/mile conversion table.

Extras:

RACES: None.

SPECIAL EVENTS: The Balsams offers special moonlight ski trips, guided tours, and clinics.

OTHER: Bring your ice skates or rent a pair. There is an ice-skating rink behind the hotel.

The hotel also features two lounges and live music and dancing, nightclub entertainment on weekends, and a plethora of activities for kids.

For American history buffs, Dixville Notch is the first place to declare its vote in presidential elections, and the hotel maintains a small gallery of presidential memorabilia.

Travel Instructions: This is not the most accessible ski area in New England, but if you're traveling in daylight, the trip has its visual rewards.

FROM BOSTON: Take I-93 north to Exit 35, then Route 3 north to Colebrook, and Route 26 east to the Balsams (you can't miss it—it's the only castle in sight). Or you can take I-95 to either Route 16 at Portsmouth (if you want to pass by Mount Washington) or Route 26 (if you've always wanted to visit Maine). Route 16 intersects Route 26 in Errol; go 22 miles west on Route 26 to the Balsams.

FROM NEW YORK: Pick up I-91 in New Haven and take it all the way up to Route 2, which is just north of the intersection of I-91 and I-93, near St. Johnsbury, Vermont. Take Route 2 east to Route 3 at Lancaster, New Hampshire. Head north on Route 3 and turn right on Route 26 at Colebrook as described above.

Bretton Woods Ski Touring Center

ROUTE 302
BRETTON WOODS, NEW HAMPSHIRE 03575

For Ski Conditions:

HOURS OF OPERATION: 8:30 A.M. to 4:30 P.M., daily

SNOW PHONE: 603/278-5181
603/278-5000 (ski lodge)

Profile:

TRAILS: Bretton Woods maintains 37 trails, totaling approximately 90 km, all of which are rolled. Sixty km are groomed and track set as required. Most trails have a skating lane, although skating is not permitted on the B & M trails. The trail system is classified as 30 percent easy, 40 percent more difficult, and 30 percent most difficult.

GROOMING: Above average to excellent. Bretton Woods has recently added a power tiller to its arsenal of grooming equipment, and consequently, is now fully equipped to handle marginal conditions. The Ammonoosuc Trail System and Mountain Road receive priority grooming, which takes about twenty hours. Many of the other trails in the Bretton Woods network require a lot of snow to be skiable, so be sure to call ahead and determine exactly which trails are open.

RENTALS: Bretton Woods rents Fischer waxless skis and also 10 pairs of Atomic waxless and regular skis, all with Salomon (SNS) bindings and Merrill boots. They also have several pairs of skating skis.

FOR WAX LOVERS: A complete supply of wax accessories is available. The waxing area is inside the ski lodge, so it is well heated. It is also well appointed, offering several work stations with ski braces.

FOOD & LODGING: There are few choices in the immediate area. A cozy snack bar at the XC center offers sandwiches, hot fast food, snacks, and beverages.

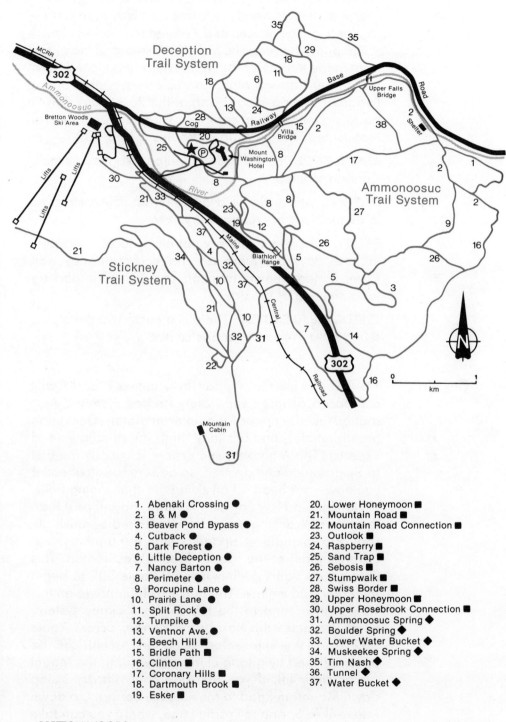

1. Abenaki Crossing ●
2. B & M ●
3. Beaver Pond Bypass ●
4. Cutback ●
5. Dark Forest ●
6. Little Deception ●
7. Nancy Barton ●
8. Perimeter ●
9. Porcupine Lane ●
10. Prairie Lane ●
11. Split Rock ●
12. Turnpike ●
13. Ventnor Ave. ●
14. Beech Hill ■
15. Bridle Path ■
16. Clinton ■
17. Coronary Hills ■
18. Dartmouth Brook ■
19. Esker ■

20. Lower Honeymoon ■
21. Mountain Road ■
22. Mountain Road Connection ■
23. Outlook ■
24. Raspberry ■
25. Sand Trap ■
26. Sebosis ■
27. Stumpwalk ■
28. Swiss Border ■
29. Upper Honeymoon ■
30. Upper Rosebrook Connection ■
31. Ammonoosuc Spring ◆
32. Boulder Spring ◆
33. Lower Water Bucket ◆
34. Muskeekee Spring ◆
35. Tim Nash ◆
36. Tunnel ◆
37. Water Bucket ◆

BRETTON WOODS
73

In addition there is Darby's Restaurant & Lounge at the Lodge at Bretton Woods, and Fabyans Station, a restaurant and lounge housed in a restored railroad station.

Although the majestic Mount Washington Hotel sits right in the middle of the trail system, it is closed from November through May. Rooms are available at the Lodge at Bretton Woods and at the Rosebrook Townhouses condominium complex. There are also several motels near the junction of Routes 3 and 302.

ALPINE FACILITIES IN AREA: Bretton Woods, Attitash, Cannon Mountain.

LESSONS: Instruction is available from PSIA instructors in all methods of cross country skiing.

SAFETY: There are courtesy patrols by local skiers during the day, but there are no end-of-the-day trail sweeps. Management monitors cars left in the parking lot at the end of the day.

CHILDCARE FACILITIES: There is a nursery at the alpine skiing area in the new sports center.

Gestalt: The 90-km Bretton Woods trail network is actually composed of three separately named systems: Ammonoosuc (beginner and intermediate), Deception (intermediate), and Stickney (high intermediates and experts). The Ammonoosuc system is usually the first to be groomed and opened, so be sure to call ahead if you have your heart set on skiing the challenging trails.

No sight in New England is more magnificent than the Mount Washington Hotel with its red Spanish tile roof and splendid veranda shimmering on the snow-covered plain at the foot of Mount Washington. This vista greets skiers as they turn off Route 302 to begin their day's adventure. The only way to improve on this view is to ascend to the top of the Stickney system, which traverses the Rosebrook Range, across Route 302 from the ski center. Such an ascent can be accomplished by a long climb or by riding the Mount Oscar chair lift. If you take the chair lift, try skiing down Mountain Road to Muskeekee Spring. Go down Muskeekee Spring to Prairie Lane, where you can take a breather as you ski over to Ammonoosuc Spring.

Take a reading of your stamina at this point: full of it, ski up to the mountain cabin at the top of the trail; half full, ski a short distance up to Boulder Spring, which loops back down; empty, head down Ammonoosuc Spring to Water Bucket, and back to the parking lot.

Advanced beginners and intermediates will definitely enjoy the following loop, which offers several scenic wonders: from the XC center headquarters take Lower Honeymoon to the Villa Bridge (vista one). Cross over the Ammonoosuc River to Bridle Path (the most boring part of this loop) and head up to Upper Falls Bridge (vista two). Go back to Tunnel Trail and ski up to Coronary Hills. Turn left on Coronary Hills and ski down to B & M and the shelter (vista three). On a clear day the shelter is a delightful picnic spot with a view of Mount Washington. After your snack, if you're looking for the steepest way down, try Coronary Hills (just the name used to scare us), a wide, mostly straight, fun downhill run. If you prefer a longer and slower return, continue on B & M to Clinton; you may either stick with Clinton until Beech Hill or jump off at Sebosis. If you choose Beech Hill, head up Dark Forest to Sebosis, which connects with Perimeter for the final return.

Bretton Woods offers an excellent contoured, waterproof map that has been recently upgraded to include trail distances.

Extras:

RACES: Bretton Woods hosts several races during the year, including biathlons; call for information.

OTHER: A pool, sauna, and Jacuzzi are available at the Lodge at Bretton Woods.

Travel Instructions:

FROM BOSTON: Take I-93 north until it temporarily terminates at Route 3. Head north on Route 3 through craggy Franconia Notch until Route 3 intersects Route 302. Turn right and go east on Route 302. The XC trails surround the first "Fantasy Land" castle on your left.

FROM NEW YORK: Take I-91 north to Route 302 east. Follow 302 to Bretton Woods.

All roads are usually well maintained.

13

Gunstock Ski Touring Center

P.O. BOX 336
LACONIA, NEW HAMPSHIRE 03247

**For Ski
Conditions:**

HOURS OF OPERATION: 8:30 A.M. to 4:30 P.M., daily

SNOW PHONE: 603/293-4341
603/293-4346

Profile:

TRAILS: Gunstock has 11 trails, totaling approximately 25 km. The entire system is rolled, and 20 km are double-track set as needed. The trails have been widened recently to accommodate skating on all but the Brook Run Trail. The trail system is classified as 30 percent easy, 40 percent more difficult, and 30 percent most difficult.

GROOMING: Excellent. Gunstock uses state-of-the-art grooming equipment.

RENTALS: Gunstock rents a variety of waxless skis, with Salomon boots and bindings, as well as a few skating and telemark skis. They do not rent waxable skis or racing skis, but they do have a few pairs of snowshoes.

FOR WAX LOVERS: A complete supply of wax accessories is available. At present skiers are asked to wax in a small unheated area, but as we write this, the entire Gunstock complex is in the midst of a multimillion dollar expansion program that includes larger quarters for the cross country ski center.

FOOD & LODGING: The cross country ski center sits adjacent to the Alpine ski lodge (150 yards), where in a reasonable facsimile of Bavarian ambience, they offer typical Alpine skier fare (cafeteria style) and après-ski conviviality and liquid spirits in the Powder Keg Lounge.

The Gunstock complex is right in the middle of the New Hampshire Lakes Region, which means that there are an abundance of lodging establishments and restaurants from which to choose. Although there are no accommodations at the skiing facility, management provides a reservation service and can usually supply a room within a 15-minute radius of the mountain.

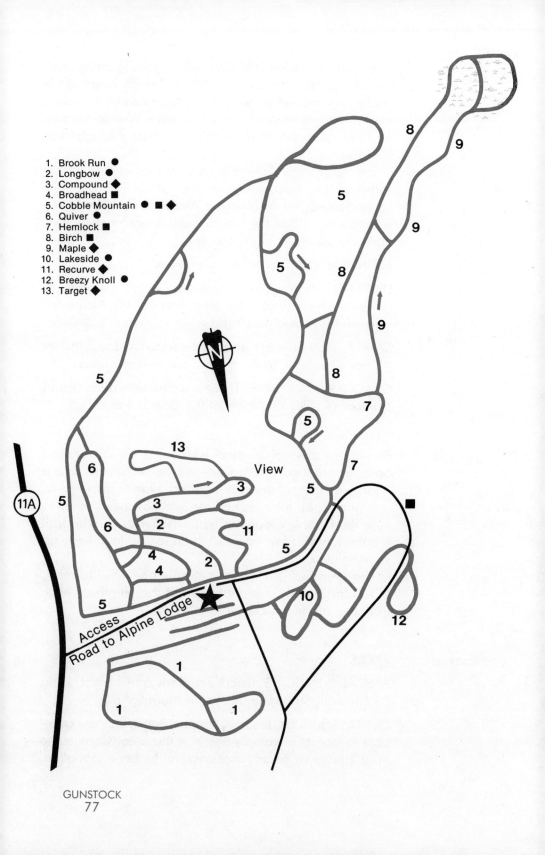

1. Brook Run ●
2. Longbow ●
3. Compound ◆
4. Broadhead ■
5. Cobble Mountain ● ■ ◆
6. Quiver ●
7. Hemlock ■
8. Birch ■
9. Maple ◆
10. Lakeside ●
11. Recurve ◆
12. Breezy Knoll ●
13. Target ◆

View

11A

Access
Road to Alpine Lodge

The Gunstock Inn is almost within walking distance of the XC center. The inn features a health club with a swimming pool, whirlpool baths, and exercise equipment; rooms with outstanding views of Lake Winnipesaukee and the surrounding mountains; and surprisingly reasonable rates.

The Christmas Tree Inn in nearby Guilford offers some of the best dining in the area. The menu is sophisticated, the ambience is pleasant, and the service is excellent (one of the few well-oiled machines that we have encountered in ski country).

ALPINE FACILITIES IN AREA: Gunstock.

LESSONS: Instruction is available in all methods of cross country skiing. Take advantage of the Alpine facility and give telemarking a whirl.

SAFETY: The trails are patrolled during the day, but they do not sweep the trails at the close of operations.

CHILDCARE FACILITIES: There is a complete nursery and childcare facility available at the downhill area.

Gestalt: Be aware that when Gunstock is crowded, the ski trails can be as frustrating as clotted arteries. So call ahead, and if a large quantity of skiers is expected, plan to arrive early.

A good loop for intermediate and advanced skiers to try is the Cobble Mountain Trail. The terrain on this trail is varied, with a few downhill thrills tossed in to keep up your enthusiasm.

The Gunstock trail map is simple and easy to read, but unfortunately does not present the length of each trail in a readily discernable manner.

Extras: **RACES:** None.

SPECIAL EVENTS: Gunstock regularly offers night skiing by candlelight, headlamps, and moonlight.

OTHER: Hot tubs, Jacuzzis, saunas, pools, etc., are available to guests of various hotels in the area. Contact the Winnipesaukee Resort Association for further information.

Travel Instructions:

FROM BOSTON: From I-93 north take exit 20 to Route 3. At Laconia, turn right on Route 11A to Gunstock.

FROM NEW YORK: Follow I-91 north to Route 9 east in Brattleboro, Vermont. Take Route 9 east to Concord, New Hampshire, pick up I-93 north, and proceed to exit 20 as described above.

All of the roads to Gunstock are usually well maintained, but Route 11A can be treacherous in icy conditions.

Jackson Ski Touring Center

JACKSON, NEW HAMPSHIRE 03846

For Ski Conditions:

HOURS OF OPERATION: The trail system is open 24 hours a day, and the office is open from 8:00 A.M. to 4:30 P.M., daily.

SNOW PHONE: 603/383-9355

LODGING: 603/383-9356

Profile:

TRAILS: Jackson maintains 60 trails, totaling approximately 203 km, of which 80 km are groomed and double-track set as required. Part of the system is always groomed for skating. Skating trails are rotated periodically. The trail system is classified as 25 percent easy, 26 percent more difficult, and 49 percent most difficult.

GROOMING: Excellent. Jackson uses state-of-the-art grooming equipment. They also know how to take advantage of the size of their system. On marginal grooming days when many XC centers refuse to groom for fear of ruining their trails for a week (i.e., warm mushy days followed by freezing nights), Jackson will close half of their system to save it for better days and risk grooming the other half to avoid disappointing their weekend patrons.

RENTALS: The Jack Frost Shop, which is attached to the Jackson Ski Touring Foundation (the nonprofit entity that maintains the trails for the village of Jackson) has 400 pairs of waxless Rossignol skis to rent, as well as an assortment of Karhu, Fischer, and Rossignol waxable skis. They come with Salomon bindings (SNS), although some skis are still mounted with 75-mm bindings. They rent Salomon boots and an assortment of 75-mm boots. They also rent skating skis, telemark skis, and new model demonstration skis.

FOR WAX LOVERS: A complete supply of wax accessories is available. The waxing area, located in the foundation of the Jackson Ski Foundation building (pardon), was intelligently renovated in 1988. The new facility includes two workbenches with ski vises, set-ups for waxing irons, and a gravel floor.

FOOD & LODGING: Thy cup runneth over! Jackson and nearby North Conway offer as many or more food and lodging possibilities than any other ski area in New England.

Try Jackson first. A dozen or so inns are located right on the Jackson trail system, so you can step directly from the inn onto your skis, ski to another inn for breakfast, another for lunch, and loop back to your bed on a different trail. This is one of the great charms of Jackson. Our favorite abode is the Nestlenook Farm Inn.

We liked the Nestlenook Inn when it was a charming funky old farm house. Five million dollars and a new proprietor later—we still like it. One of the stated goals of the Inn is to make its patrons feel like they have stepped into a Currier & Ives painting. The new Nestlenook boasts a sculpted meandering ice skating pond with heated warming gazebo (open day and night), as well as day and night sleigh rides. The Inn features a plethora of custom hand-crafted Victoriana, Jacuzzis in all the guest rooms, and one of the best restaurants in the Mt. Washington Valley. With only seven rooms, Nestlenook's rates are at the high end of snow country's scale. More modestly priced is the recently built Lodge at Jackson Village. If you're tired of discovering that "country inn" is a euphemism for drafty windows, antiquated heating, and unreliable hot water, the Lodge is a sure bet. It's a modern facility replete with cable TV, refrigerators in each room, and accommodations for the disabled.

The variety of high-quality cuisine in the area is also astounding—ranging from French, to Austrian, to traditional Mexican fare. Everybody's favorite in the center of Jackson is the Wildcat Inn, which offers solid meals in the dining room and the perfect post-ski ambience in the adjacent tavern.

ALPINE FACILITIES IN AREA: Attitash, Wildcat Mountain, Mount Cranmore, Black Mountain.

LESSONS: Instruction is available in all methods of cross country skiing.

SAFETY: The trails are patrolled during the day, but not at night.

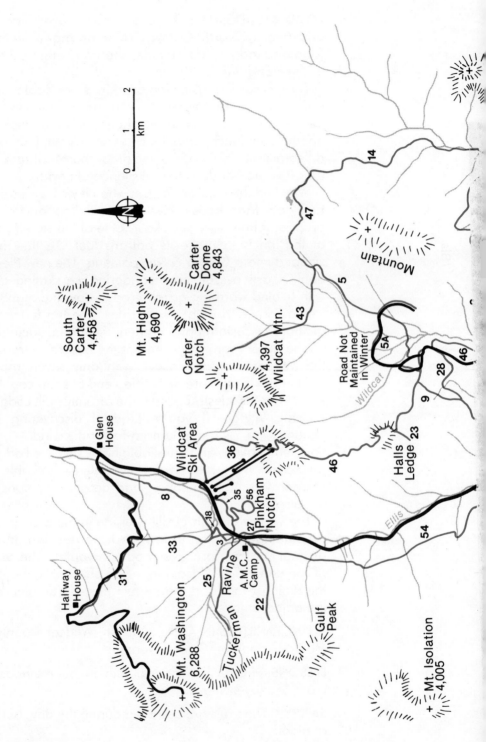

South Carter
4,458

Mt. Hight
4,690

Carter Dome
4,843

Carter Notch

Wildcat Mtn.
4,397

Wildcat

Mountain

14

47

5

43

5A

46

28

9

Halls Ledge

23

Road Not Maintained in Winter

Glen House

Wildcat Ski Area

36

35

56

Pinkham Notch

46

Ellis

54

8

18

27

3

33

A.M.C. Camp

Halfway House

31

25

Tuckerman Ravine

22

Gulf Peak

Mt. Washington
6,288

Mt. Isolation
4,005

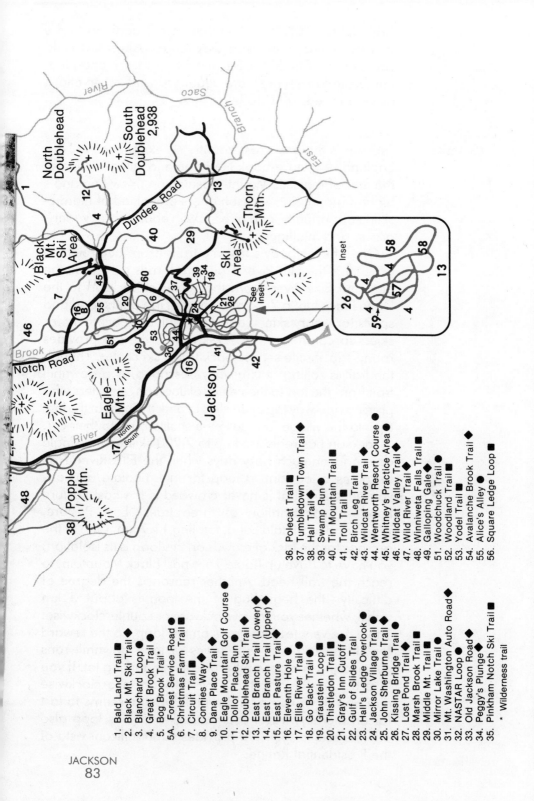

1. Bald Land Trail ■
2. Black Mt. Ski Trail ◆
3. Blanchard Loop ●
4. Great Brook Trail ●
5. Bog Brook Trail*
5A. Forest Service Road ●
6. Christmas Farm Trail ■
7. Circuit Trail ■
8. Connies Way ◆
9. Dana Place Trail ■
10. Eagle Mountain Golf Course ●
11. Dollof Place Run ■
12. Doublehead Ski Trail ◆
13. East Branch Trail (Lower) ◆
14. East Branch Trail (Upper) ◆
15. East Pasture Trail ■
16. Eleventh Hole ●
17. Ellis River Trail ■
18. Go Back Trail ■
19. Graustein Loop ■
20. Thistledon Trail ■
21. Gray's Inn Cutoff ●
22. Gulf of Slides Trail ◆
23. Hall's Ledge Overlook ●
24. Jackson Village Trail ■
25. John Sherburne Trail ◆
26. Kissing Bridge Trail ●
27. Lost Pond Trail ◆
28. Marsh Brook Trail ■
29. Middle Mt. Trail ■
30. Mirror Lake Trail ■
31. Mt. Washington Auto Road ◆
32. NASTAR Loop ■
33. Old Jackson Road ◆
34. Peggy's Plunge ■
35. Pinkham Notch Ski Trail ■

36. Polecat Trail ■
37. Tumbledown Town Trail ◆
38. Hall Trail ■
39. Swamp Run ●
40. Tin Mountain Trail ■
41. Troll Trail ■
42. Birch Leg Trail ●
43. Wildcat River Trail ◆
44. Wentworth Resort Course ●
45. Whitney's Practice Area ●
46. Wildcat Valley Trail ◆
47. Wild River Trail ◆
48. Winniweta Falls Trail ◆
49. Galloping Gale ■
51. Woodchuck Trail ■
52. Woodland Trail ●
53. Yodel Trail ■
54. Avalanche Brook Trail ◆
55. Alice's Alley ■
56. Square Ledge Loop ■

* Wilderness trail

CHILDCARE FACILITIES: Another recent addition to the Jackson scene is Jackson Day Care, a licensed child care center. Children over one year old are accepted, immunization records are required, and reservations are requested. 603/383-6134.

Gestalt: Jackson is the best cross country ski experience in New England! A picture-book New England village sitting at the foot of majestic Mount Washington (New England's highest mountain), Jackson offers every kind of Nordic-skiing opportunity, and offers it with abundance, variety, grace, and intelligence.

One of everybody's favorite trails (from beginners to experts) is the Ellis River Trail, which rolls alongside the beautiful Ellis River, from the center of Jackson to the Dana Place Inn, a 7.7-km jaunt. The inn offers food and spirits for weary skiers, and as a further inducement for skiers to commit to the 7.7-km trail, the inn provides round-trip shuttle service back to the ski center. Though the trail is rolling, it is usually described as a downhill trail from the inn to the center of Jackson, so skiers who prefer a one-way trip often elect to park their car at the inn, ski into the village, and take the shuttle back to their car.

Jackson has registered up to 2,200 skiers on a single day, and on such busy days when the Ellis River Trail becomes a log jam, a loop for intermediate and advanced skiers that is never crowded is the East Pasture Loop—a combination of three trails, East Pasture, Woodland, and Bald Land, totaling 11.7 km. One of the reasons for the lack of crowds on this loop is its isolation; you have to drive up Route 16B, past Black Mountain, to reach the trail head. Another reason is the degree of difficulty—the beginning of the loop is about 3 km uphill, whether you travel clockwise or counterclockwise. There are very few flat areas on this loop, so the reward for all the climbing is a series of long downhill runs culminating in a downhill cruise to the parking lot. If you love a hairy hairpin turn, try this loop in a clockwise direction. If you savor a downhill run that seems to last for an eternity, travel counterclockwise. This loop also offers a scenic spur that provides a magnificent vista of the Presidential Range.

A third favorite loop incorporates the Hot Chocolate Circuit, a group of trails that maximizes the number of inns one can visit in search of the perfect watering hole. Although skiers can concoct a Hot Chocolate Circuit to match their abilities, we recommend the following loop for intermediate and advanced skiers: start behind the Wildcat Tavern and take the Jackson Village Trail (#24) to Swamp Run (#39). A short ski down Swamp Run terminates at Graustein Loop (#19). Turn left and go straight up—a very steep ascent rewarded by a delightful, curvy, downhill run that returns to the Jackson Village Trail. At this juncture you can choose between taking a short trip to the Thorn Hill Lodge (which will require retracing your steps to reenter the circuit) or continuing on the Jackson Village Trail to the Christmas Farm Trail (#6). Christmas Farm Trail is mainly an ascent to the Christmas Farm Inn, which is happy to reward your climb with food and spirits, but the best reward for your efforts appears when you cross Route 16B to continue the trail and glimpse the breathtaking sight of the Eagle Mountain House, a sprawling old Victorian hotel (that was one of the location candidates for Stanley Kubrick's classic "The Shining") set against the backdrop of snowcapped Mount Washington. When you've had your fill of the view, try a 1988 addition to the network, The Wave (#60). Like its name, The Wave is an undulating, fun loop that was designed for skaters but is also groomed for classic skiers. Then ski over to the Eagle Mountain House, where once again, skiers' fare is available inside. There are many ways back to the center of the village, but our favorite, as well as one of our favorite downhill runs in the system, is Galloping Gale (#49), a fantastic trail beginning with a short climb that quickly leads to a series of downhill runs with tight curves and just the right number of resting spots to allow you to catch your breath and collect your concentration. The entire loop described above is approximately 9 km.

It is worth noting that Jackson offers three different guides to their trail system: a free handout that, while superior to many touring maps, offers the minimum amount of information required to understand such a vast and complex system; a waterproof topographical map that contains brief descriptions of each trail; and a guidebook with more detailed descriptions of the Jackson experience. We feel that the topographical map is a good investment.

Extras: RACES: Jackson hosts a number of races each year that can range from the NCAA Championships to World Nordic Championships for the Disabled to competition for first-time racers.

OTHER: Available in Jackson or North Conway is just about any "goodie" you would expect to find in a major ski resort: hot tubs, skating rinks, heated swimming pools, saunas, exercise facilities, etc.

Travel Instructions: FROM BOSTON: The quickest way to go, traffic permitting, is to take I-95 north to Portsmouth, New Hampshire, where you pick up the Spaulding Turnpike and Route 16, which goes all the way to Jackson. Turn right at the covered bridge. If you anticipate crowded highways, you may want to take I-93 north to Lincoln, New Hampshire, and the Kancamagus Highway (Route 112), which terminates at Route 16 near Conway. Under normal conditions this route takes 3 to 3½ hours, but be aware that the Kancamagus is treacherous when covered with snow.

FROM NEW YORK: Take I-91 north to Route 302 east. Take Route 302 all the way to Glen, New Hampshire, then head north on Route 16 to Jackson.

15

Norsk Ski Touring Center

ROUTE 11
NEW LONDON, NEW HAMPSHIRE 03257

For Ski Conditions:

HOURS OF OPERATION: 8:30 A.M. to 5:00 P.M., daily

SKI REPORT: 800/42-NORSK

SHOP & INFORMATION: 603/526-4685

LODGING: 603/526-6040

Profile:

TRAILS: Norsk has 19 trails, totaling 80 km, all of which are groomed and track set as needed. To derive the 80 km distance each trail was measured from trailhead to finish, including overlapping loops. Total non-overlapped trail distance is 44.8 km. Skating is permitted on five trails (20 km). All of the trails are designed for one-way skiing. Norsk classifies its system as 30 percent easy, 45 percent more difficult, and 25 percent most difficult.

GROOMING: Excellent. Norsk uses state-of-the-art grooming equipment. They always seem to be able to provide skiable terrain on those frustrating days when many other areas can't, and in 1989 they added snow-making equipment.

RENTALS: Norsk rents Trak waxless skis with SNS bindings, Salomon boots, a few pairs of waxable skis, and a few pairs of skating skis.

FOR WAX LOVERS: Norsk offers a complete supply of wax accessories. There is an unheated waxing shed near the ski shop, but waxing in the heated ski shop is not prohibited.

FOOD & LODGING: Norsk is part of the Lake Sunapee Country Club and Inn complex, which includes a very good restaurant and lounge, and a charming inn. In addition, the quaint college town of New London (a five-minute drive from Norsk) offers a variety of lodging and eating establishments.

The favorite casual restaurant in the center of New London is Peter Christian's Tavern (P.C.'s), which offers a large, varied menu and the quintessential winter ambience.

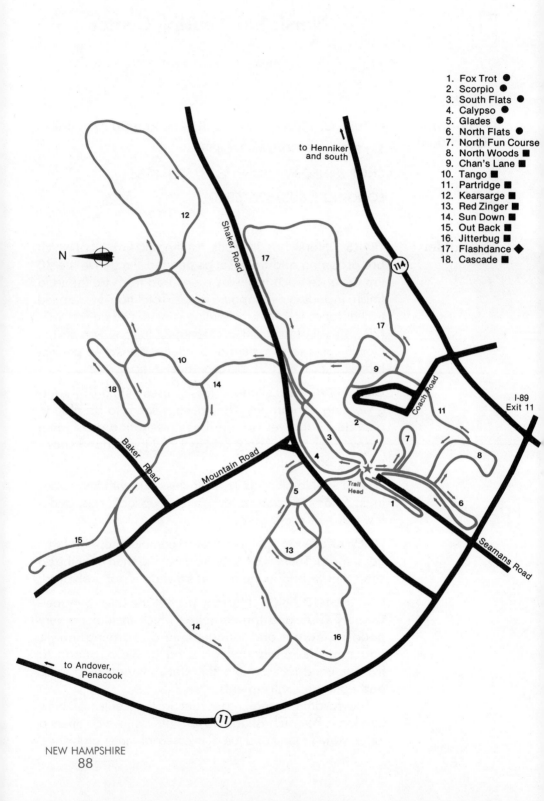

1. Fox Trot ●
2. Scorpio ●
3. South Flats ●
4. Calypso ●
5. Glades ●
6. North Flats ●
7. North Fun Course
8. North Woods ■
9. Chan's Lane ■
10. Tango ■
11. Partridge ■
12. Kearsarge ■
13. Red Zinger ■
14. Sun Down ■
15. Out Back ■
16. Jitterbug ■
17. Flashdance ◆
18. Cascade ■

to Henniker
and south

I-89
Exit 11

Shaker Road

Coach Road

Baker Road

Mountain Road

Seamans Road

Trail Head

to Andover,
Penacook

NEW HAMPSHIRE
88

ALPINE FACILITIES IN AREA: King Ridge, Mount Sunapee.

LESSONS: Instruction is available in all methods of cross country skiing.

SAFETY: Although there are no regular ski patrols during the day, all trails are swept at the end of each day by Norsk instructors.

CHILDCARE FACILITIES: None.

Gestalt:

Norsk sits at the foot of Mount Kearsarge—not a particularly impressive mountain compared with other peaks noted in this book. Norsk's trails do not offer thrilling vistas, and if you are an advanced skier, you will find few challenges on these trails. So why do we regard Norsk as one of the top ski areas in New England?

The trails at Norsk are meticulously groomed (usually by the proprietor), intelligently designed (given the limits of the terrain), and well marked and mapped. When nature is uncooperative and the snow cover begins to dwindle, the Norsk staff can be found shoveling snow out of the woods onto the trails. In addition, to stimulate its devoted patrons, Norsk seems to add something new to its trail system each year.

Cross Country Skier called Norsk a family place. To accommodate families, there is plenty of interesting skiing right around the inn that will delight beginners and toddlers without exhausting them far away from the comforts of a warm fire and hot chocolate.

If you are a more adventurous skier, you may want to try the 11 km trek to Robb's Trail Hut and back. Take South to Tango to Sundown (not shown on map), which leads to the Outback Spur. The mid-trek reward at the end of the 1 km Outback Spur is Robb's heated warming hut featuring hot chocolate, chili, and trail snacks. Return to the inn on Sundown and South Loop. All of these trails are rolling and pleasant and should not prove difficult for an intermediate skier to negotiate.

The most challenging spots in the Norsk system are the narrow twisting drops on El Gato, Flashdance, and Jitterbug. The thrill is brief but memorable.

Extras: RACES: The annual 10-km Governor's Race is held at the end of January.

SPECIAL EVENTS: Norsk offers a full winter calendar of activities, including moonlight tours, a New Year's Eve ski tour, a backcountry ski over Mount Kearsarge, telemark clinics at Pine Ridge, group skis to a wood-fired sauna in the forest, and the New London Winterfest.

Travel Instructions: FROM BOSTON: Take I-93 north to I-89 north, exit 11. Go 1½ miles north on Route 11 and take the first right past Grey House restaurant.

FROM NEW YORK: Follow I-91 north to I-89 south, exit 11; proceed as outlined above.

All of the roads to Norsk are excellently maintained during snowstorms.

16

Waterville Valley
Cross Country Center

WATERVILLE VALLEY, NEW HAMPSHIRE 03215

For Ski Conditions:

HOURS OF OPERATION: 8:30 A.M. to 4:30 P.M., weekends; 9:00 A.M. to 4:30 P.M., weekdays

SNOW PHONE: 603/236-4144
603/236-8311

Profile:

TRAILS: Waterville Valley has 20 trails, totaling approximately 70 km. The entire system is groomed and double-track set daily (if required). Although all trails are groomed for skating, the Lycra set is usually encouraged to use White Mountain Criterion, a 6.5-km expert trail that is often used as a race course. The trail system is classified as 30 percent easy, 50 percent more difficult, and 20 percent most difficult.

GROOMING: Nobody does it better. Waterville Valley uses state-of-the-art grooming equipment. "Angry" Al Swan provides the best skate-groomed trails in New England. We have even witnessed ski instructors shoveling snow out of the woods to cover worn spots in critical sections of downhill runs.

RENTALS: Waterville Valley rents Trak and Karhu equipment exclusively—waxless and telemark skis, boots, bindings, and poles. They do not rent waxable classic skis, but skating skis are available.

FOR WAX LOVERS: A complete supply of wax accessories is available. The waxing room is located in the basement of the new cross country center facility. It is well heated and has an ample supply of workbenches.

FOOD & LODGING: Though many small towns in the area offer food and lodging, Waterville Valley is a self-contained destination resort. There is not much in Waterville Valley that is not owned by "The Corporation." In addition to a community of condominiums (which can be rented), hotels, and restaurants of reasonably harmonious architecture, The Corporation has

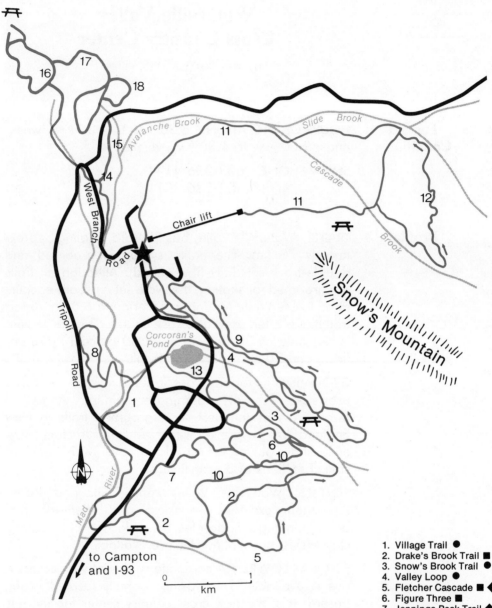

Chair lift

Avalanche Brook

Slide Brook

Cascade Brook

West Branch Road

Tripoli Road

Corcoran's Pond

Snow's Mountain

Mad River

to Campton
and I-93

0   km   1

N

1. Village Trail ●
2. Drake's Brook Trail ■
3. Snow's Brook Trail ●
4. Valley Loop ●
5. Fletcher Cascade ■ ◆
6. Figure Three ■
7. Jennings Peak Trail ◆
8. Mad River Trail ■
9. White Mountain Criterior
10. Joe's Choice ■
11. Snow's Mountain Trail ■
12. Cascade Brook Trail ■
13. Pond Loop ●
14. Osceola Look ● ■
15. Greely Path ●
16. John Deer ■
17. Moose Run ●
18. Wicked Easy ●

recently constructed a Disney-like, New England town square, complete with restaurants (The Red Stallion and The Yacht Club), a huge new luxury hotel (The Golden Eagle Lodge), shops, and the cross country center.

There are also two eateries on the trails. The Finish Line offers a tasty variety of finger food and entrées (the menu seems to change from year to year), as well as spirits. However, The Finish Line also services Alpine skiers from Snow's Mountain (the chair lift is right next to the restaurant), so it is not uncommon to have to wait for a table.

In the winter of 1985–86, The Corporation opened Bull Hill Cabin, a rustic soup-sandwich-pastry-and-hot-beverage place that sits at the beginning of Valley Loop and White Mountain Criterion Trail and should be visited only on cross country skis.

One nearby town worth noting is Campton (about 15–20 minutes from Waterville Valley and right off I-93), which contains several small inns and restaurants.

ALPINE FACILITIES IN AREA: There are two developed mountains at Waterville Valley: Mount Tecumseh and Snow's Mountain.

LESSONS: Instruction is available in all methods of cross country skiing. An excellent practice area near the ski shop has many double tracks for diagonal striders and rolled areas for skaters.

SAFETY: The trails are patrolled during the day and all trails are swept by 4:30 P.M.

CHILDCARE FACILITIES: Available at the Mount Tecumseh skiing area, two miles from the cross country center.

Gestalt:

Only two hours from downtown Boston, Waterville Valley is frequently used as a day-trip destination by skiers from that area. For pure skiing pleasure Waterville Valley can't be beat. Over the past few years they have developed the best skating trail network in New England.

One of the attractions is that the downhill runs are quick, curvy, and fun. A ski-magazine writer, who as a novice loathed Waterville Valley, bittersweetly remembers the "infamous hairpin turn where I would frequently launch myself into hyperspace." It is fair to say that this trail system offers more to intermediate and advanced skiers than to beginners.

If you're a skater, head for White Mountain Criterion, a one-way loop, groomed for skating. Frequently used as a race course, a third of this trail is flat; a third, uphill; and a third, downhill—with a rolling screamer at the end.

On the other side of the trail system are Snow's Mountain Trail and its appendage Cascade Brook, wonderful trails for intermediate and advanced skiers. Snow's Mountain Trail can be accessed by either skiing up and down the same stretch of snow (it doesn't form a loop) or by taking Osceola to Livermore Road to the bridge at Slide Brook (a longer, but varied approach). The good news is that skiing up and down Snow's Mountain has never seemed boring because the character of the trail changes substantially—from a long, but not too rigorous, uphill climb to a long downhill run that alternates between the challenges of speed and tight turns and the joys of "cruise control." Another piece of good news is that the summit of Snow's Mountain Trail can be reached by chair lift; however, we have always preferred the climb. Skiing up Snow's Mountain Trail has its benefits: an unexpected, exciting, S-curved downhill run about one quarter of the way up the mountain and romantic bridge crossings of picturesque Cascade Brook that are bypassed too quickly on the descent. Another benefit of climbing on a sunny day is taking a snack break at the summit, where a mysterious deck located just below the chair lift shack (it appears to be an abandoned project) is an ideal spot to rest and get a winter tan.

The best part of this ski is the downhill side of Cascade Brook, a loop off Snow's Mountain Trail, which we usually attempt after coming down from the summit. Be aware that you should not begin this trail if you are already fatigued from the ascent of Snow's Mountain; because the beginning of Cascade Brook is all uphill, the rest of the trail is a challenging descent. But the descent is probably the most fun downhill run at Waterville Valley. It begins with a series of short, rolling ups and downs and climaxes with a long series of interlocking curves and hairpin turns. From the end of Cascade Brook, put on "cruise control" back to the ski shop, except during one short, steep downhill just before the last bridge over Cascade Brook and one final, fun descent at the very end of the trail.

Waterville Valley also has one of the best map and trail-marking systems.

Extras:

RACES: Waterville Valley hosts an annual triathlon, the White Mountain Chase (a part of the Great American Ski Chase), and many other USSA-sanctioned races that vary from year to year. In the past Waterville Valley has hosted the Nationals, NORAM, World Junior Championship Tryouts, and World Cup races. There are also Bill Koch races for children and marathons.

OTHER: This place is loaded with goodies: indoor and outdoor skating rinks, heated outdoor-indoor swimming pool, and a complete sports center that features tennis courts, an Olympic-size swimming pool, indoor track, weight room, racquetball, squash, and saunas.

Travel Instructions:

FROM BOSTON: Take I-93 north to exit 28; follow signs to Waterville Valley (about 10 miles).

FROM NEW YORK: Follow I-91 north to Brattleboro, Vermont. Take Route 9 east to I-89 east. At Concord, New Hampshire, pick up I-93 and proceed to exit 28 as described above.

All roads are well maintained.

Windblown Ski Touring

R.F.D. 2, BOX 669
NEW IPSWICH, NEW HAMPSHIRE 03071

For Ski Conditions:

HOURS OF OPERATION: 9:00 A.M. to 5:00 P.M., daily

SNOW PHONE: 603/878-2869

Profile:

TRAILS: Windblown has 12 to 27 trails (depending on how you want to count them), totaling approximately 32 km, all of which are groomed and track set as needed. In the winter of 1985–86, less than 1 percent of the skiers at Windblown were skaters. By the following season, the number had grown to 15 percent. All of the trails have been widened to at least eight feet to accommodate a Tucker Sno-Cat. Skating is permitted on approximately two thirds of the system. A 1-km loop, illuminated at night and widened to 16 feet to accommodate skaters and two sets of double tracks, has been outfitted recently with snowmaking equipment to provide skiable terrain when the snow gods are having an off year. The trail system is classified as 30 percent easy, 40 percent more difficult, and 30 percent most difficult.

GROOMING: Above average. Management is very conscientious about grooming, but their grooming equipment is a shade below state-of-the-art. On the days we skied Windblown we were very satisfied with the grooming.

RENTALS: Windblown rents Fischer and Trak waxless skis, all of which are mounted with Salomon (SNS) bindings, matched with Salomon boots. They also rent skate skis and snowshoes.

FOR WAX LOVERS: A complete selection of wax accessories is available. Waxing is accomplished in a rustic wood-stove-heated room that also functions as an area for respite.

FOOD & LODGING: In the middle of the trail system, within an easy ski for all levels of skiers, is a rest cabin that functions as a rental unit at night. The wood-stove-heated, gas-lit cabin can accommodate up to 12 skiers at an extraordinarily reasonable price, but don't expect

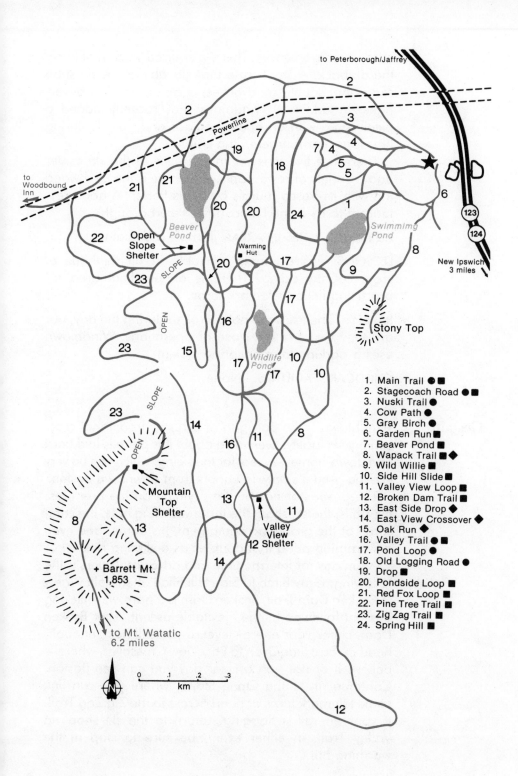

to Peterborough/Jaffrey

Powerline

to Woodbound Inn

2

2

2

3

7

19

7

4

4

18

5

5

1

★

6

123

124

New Ipswich
3 miles

21

21

20

20

Beaver
Pond

Open
Slope
Shelter

22

Warming
Hut

Swimming
Pond

24

8

23

SLOPE

20

17

9

OPEN

16

17

Stony Top

23

15

17

Wildlife
Pond

10

17

10

23

SLOPE

14

OPEN

16

11

8

Mountain
Top
Shelter

8

13

13

11

+ Barrett Mt.
1,853

12

Valley
View
Shelter

14

to Mt. Watatic
6.2 miles

0   .1   .2   .3
km

N

1. Main Trail ●■
2. Stagecoach Road ●■
3. Nuski Trail ●
4. Cow Path ●
5. Gray Birch ●
6. Garden Run ■
7. Beaver Pond ■
8. Wapack Trail ■◆
9. Wild Willie ■
10. Side Hill Slide ■
11. Valley View Loop ■
12. Broken Dam Trail ■
13. East Side Drop ◆
14. East View Crossover ◆
15. Oak Run ◆
16. Valley Trail ●■
17. Pond Loop ●
18. Old Logging Road ●
19. Drop ■
20. Pondside Loop ■
21. Red Fox Loop ■
22. Pine Tree Trail ■
23. Zig Zag Trail ■
24. Spring Hill ■

WINDBLOWN
97

modern conveniences. This is a civilized version of life in the outback. A small café that sits above the ski shop serves hot soups, sandwiches, cookies, and hot beverages. In addition, Windblown has recently added a picnic shed with an open fireplace and grill, featuring hot dogs, hamburgers, and chili.

There are five inns within 10 miles of the ski center and a variety of restaurants. A favorite is the Birchwood Inn with its fresco murals by Rufus Porter. A good restaurant to try is the Latacarta in Peterborough.

ALPINE FACILITIES IN AREA: Temple Mountain.

LESSONS: Instruction is available in all methods of cross country skiing. There is an excellent area for practicing linked telemark turns.

SAFETY: The trails are not patrolled during the day, nor are they swept at the close of operations. Windblown uses a parking lot monitoring system.

CHILDCARE FACILITIES: None.

Gestalt: Windblown is the paragon of a rustic, traditional cross country ski facility. Everything about this place is laid back and down-home—except for the skiing, which can be very exciting. And it's only 1½ hours from downtown Boston.

The proprietor has built everything on the premises: the trails, the ski shop, the three warming huts, the café, some of the grooming equipment, his home, and even a swimming pond that doubles as a skating rink.

A fun day for intermediate and advanced skiers is the following: Gray Birch to Side Hill Slide, then Valley View to Broken Dam Trail. Broken Dam is a narrow, rollicking descent followed by the inevitable ascent. After Broken Dam, check your energy level. If you still have enough, head up East Side Drop to East View Crossover, where—believe it or not—on a clear day you can see Boston. Continue on to the Open Slope, where you can link some telemark turns or head across to the Zig Zag Trail. If your energy is flagging, return to the ski shop via Valley Trail. In either event, be sure to stop at the warming hut.

At first glance Windblown appears to have a good trail map (though it doesn't include the length of trails). Once you are actually out in the system, however, the myriad of short trails and related intersections becomes confusing. To counteract this situation, management has posted water-repellent trail maps at every intersection.

Extras:

RACES: None.

SPECIAL EVENTS: Hour-long catered sleigh rides are conducted on weekends and holidays. They occasionally offer lighted night skiing and guided moonlight tours.

Travel Instructions:

FROM BOSTON: Take Route 2 west, then Route 13 north to Townsend. In Townsend take Route 119 west to Route 124 (northwest), which eventually runs right by Windblown, near New Ipswich. Be alert! The intersection of routes 119 and 124, which is about two miles beyond Townsend, is marked by only a "New Ipswich" sign.

FROM NEW YORK: Go to Boston and proceed as outlined above or take I-91 north to Route 2 east in Greenfield, Massachusetts. Take Route 2 to Route 202 north; in Jaffrey turn right on Route 124 and head for Windblown.

Although the roads to Windblown are progressively narrower, they are not appreciably steep, winding, or treacherous.

Vermont

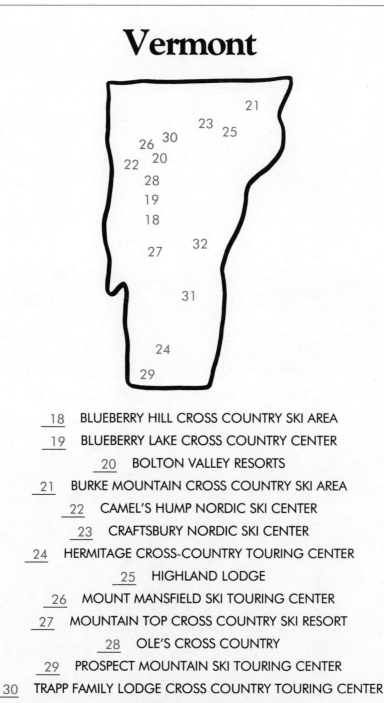

18   BLUEBERRY HILL CROSS COUNTRY SKI AREA

19   BLUEBERRY LAKE CROSS COUNTRY CENTER

20   BOLTON VALLEY RESORTS

21   BURKE MOUNTAIN CROSS COUNTRY SKI AREA

22   CAMEL'S HUMP NORDIC SKI CENTER

23   CRAFTSBURY NORDIC SKI CENTER

24   HERMITAGE CROSS-COUNTRY TOURING CENTER

25   HIGHLAND LODGE

26   MOUNT MANSFIELD SKI TOURING CENTER

27   MOUNTAIN TOP CROSS COUNTRY SKI RESORT

28   OLE'S CROSS COUNTRY

29   PROSPECT MOUNTAIN SKI TOURING CENTER

30   TRAPP FAMILY LODGE CROSS COUNTRY TOURING CENTER

31   VIKING SKI TOURING CENTRE

32   WOODSTOCK SKI TOURING CENTER

Blueberry Hill
Cross Country Ski Area

GOSHEN, VERMONT 05733

For Ski Conditions:

HOURS OF OPERATION: 8:00 A.M. to 5:00 P.M., daily

SNOW PHONE: 802/247-6735
802/247-6535
800/448-0707

Profile:

TRAILS: Blueberry Hill has 10 trails, totaling approximately 70 km, 15 km of which are ungroomed and unplowed roads. All of the groomed trails are a minimum of 12 feet wide to accommodate skating and are rolled and track set as needed to allow for skating and diagonal stride. The trail system is classified as 14 percent easy, 76 percent more difficult, and 10 percent most difficult.

GROOMING: Excellent. Blueberry Hill uses state-of-the-art grooming equipment. The people at Blueberry Hill take a very serious approach to this sport and its trends; they are trying to help the average skier explore the benefits of skating by orienting their trail system toward this relatively new technique, without making second-class citizens out of those who prefer the traditional methods.

RENTALS: Blueberry Hill rents Fischer waxless skis with SNS bindings, Salomon boots, and Exel poles. They do not rent waxable skis.

FOR WAX LOVERS: A complete supply of wax accessories is available. Waxing is allowed in a section of the wood-stove-heated ski center.

FOOD & LODGING: The ski center offers soup for free from 12:00 to 2:00 P.M. You can also purchase a limited variety of trail snacks.

The best way to experience the Blueberry Hill Cross Country Ski Area is to stay at the Blueberry Hill Inn, for which the words *quaint* and *friendly* must have been invented. Easier said than done, however. The inn has

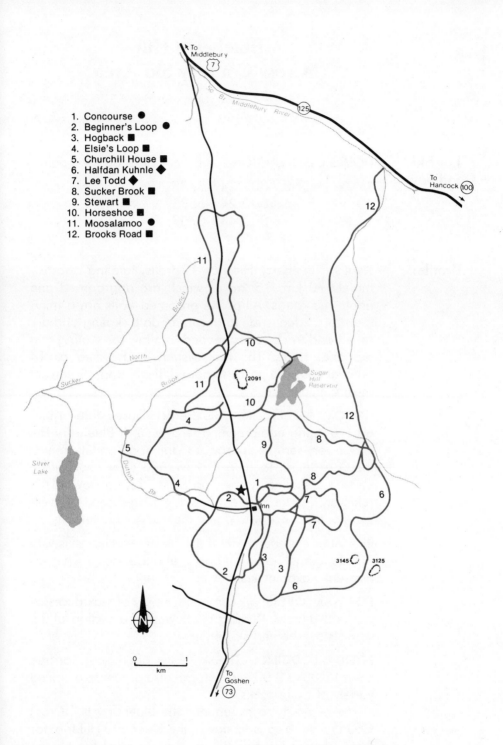

1. Concourse ●
2. Beginner's Loop ●
3. Hogback ■
4. Elsie's Loop ■
5. Churchill House ■
6. Halfdan Kuhnle ◆
7. Lee Todd ◆
8. Sucker Brook ■
9. Stewart ■
10. Horseshoe ■
11. Moosalamoo ●
12. Brooks Road ■

To Middlebury (7)

So. Br. Middlebury River

(125)

To Hancock (100)

12

11

Branch

North

Sucker

Brook

11

2091

Sugar Hill Reservoir

10

10

4

9

8

5

Silver Lake

Dutton Bk.

4

1

2

8

12

6

Inn

7

7

3

6

3

3145

3125

2

6

N

0   1
km

To Goshen (73)

only 12 rooms, and one is advised to make reservations six months in advance.

For the lucky ones who find space at the inn, the experience is well worth the advanced planning. The rooms are all well appointed. Sumptuous breakfasts and dinners are served family style, with all of the guests seated at two long tables, in a rustic dining room with a large, well-stoked fireplace. Hot beverages, cookies, and the like are available all day, with guests encouraged to wander into the country kitchen to see what's coming out of the oven.

If there are no rooms available at the inn, the village of Brandon, which also boasts several fine inns and restaurants, is close at hand.

ALPINE FACILITIES IN AREA: There are none within a 20-mile radius. The nearest facilities are Killington and Pico Peak.

LESSONS: Instruction is available in all methods of cross country skiing except telemarking.

SAFETY: The trails are not swept at the end of the day, nor are they patrolled during operating hours. A parking lot check is made at day's end.

CHILDCARE FACILITIES: Yes.

CONNECTED TO THE CATAMOUNT TRAIL: Yes.

Gestalt:

"Friendly" is a significant theme at this place. We have never encountered a more cheerful and friendly group than the staff that services both the skiers and the patrons of the inn. This of course enhances the pleasure of skiing Blueberry Hill, as does the ability to step straight from the inn onto the ski trails.

The trail system is best suited to intermediate skiers, but advanced and novice skiers will not feel slighted.

The following loop is a favorite intermediate ski, and is also part of the American Ski Chase racecourse: starting from the inn, go up and around Hogback Mountain on the trail of the same name. At marker 29 Hogback intersects Lee Todd Trail. Turn right on Lee Todd Trail and ski up and down the side of Romance Mountain until you come to marker 19, which denotes the intersection of Sucker Brook Trail. Go right on

Sucker Brook and continue a rolling ski until you reach marker 33. Go left at the marker (you will still be on Sucker Brook), and roll on to marker 35, where you can return to the inn on Stewart Trail.

In December 1986, Blueberry Hill unveiled a long-awaited, first-class trail map, a huge improvement over the previous edition. However, the map still lacks length-of-trail information.

Extras:

RACES: Each year Blueberry Hill hosts a 60-km marathon. Another annual event is "the pig race," a 10-km rite of spring that attracts elite skiers as well as citizen racers ranging in age from 8 to 70. The race features a whole roast pig and other delectables—served after the race—a square dance, costumes, pig medallions for the participants, and fiendish obstacles during the race. A definite hoot.

OTHER: They also sponsor waxing clinics, seminars, guided tours, and night skiing with head lamps.

Travel Instructions:

FROM BOSTON: Take I-93 north to I-89 west, exit 1, and follow Route 4 west to Rutland. Go north on Route 7 to Brandon, east on Route 73 to Goshen, and left at the town hall. Look for signs to Blueberry Hill. When you look at a map, this may seem like a roundabout way to get there. We have tried what seemed to be shorter routes and found them to be snow-packed, steep, and full of curves.

FROM NEW YORK: From I-87 north take Route 4 east to Rutland; then follow Route 7 north to Brandon and proceed as outlined above.

Routes 4 and 7 are usually well maintained during snowstorms; however, once you leave the state highways, you must have a vehicle that can handle snow-covered roads. This is especially true of the last few miles to the inn. Call ahead for road conditions.

19

Blueberry Lake
Cross Country Center

PLUNKTON ROAD
EAST WARREN, VERMONT 05674

For Ski Conditions:

HOURS OF OPERATION: 9:00 A.M. to 5:00 P.M., daily

SNOW PHONE: 802/496-6687

Profile:

TRAILS: Blueberry Lake has 10 trails, measuring 34.85 km, all of which are groomed and double-track set as needed—except for the 4.9-km Overlook Trail, which is left in its natural state. The trail system is classified as 33 percent easy, 37 percent more difficult, and 30 percent most difficult.

GROOMING: Above average. Blueberry Lake's grooming equipment borders on state of the art; a few pieces of homemade equipment (principally a powder maker) are tossed into the mix. On marginal days the most interesting trails are difficult to groom with this equipment, so call ahead and request specific trail conditions.
   During the snow drought that plagued central Vermont in the winter of 1988–1989, Blueberry Lake initiated a "snow farming" policy—scooping snow from the lake and open fields and distributing it on the trails with a manure spreader—allowing them to offer respectable skiing when many areas were closed. Snow farming proved so successful that Blueberry Lake continued this practice as a form of grooming insurance. In addition, they offer 5 km of artificial snow—before Christmas, temperatures permitting.

RENTALS: Blueberry Lake has a limited amount of rental equipment: 30 pairs of Rossignol waxless skis and 10 pairs of assorted waxable skis—all mounted with 50-mm bindings and matched with Alpina boots. No racing skis are available.

FOR WAX LOVERS: A modest selection of wax accessories is available. There is a heated shed for waxing.

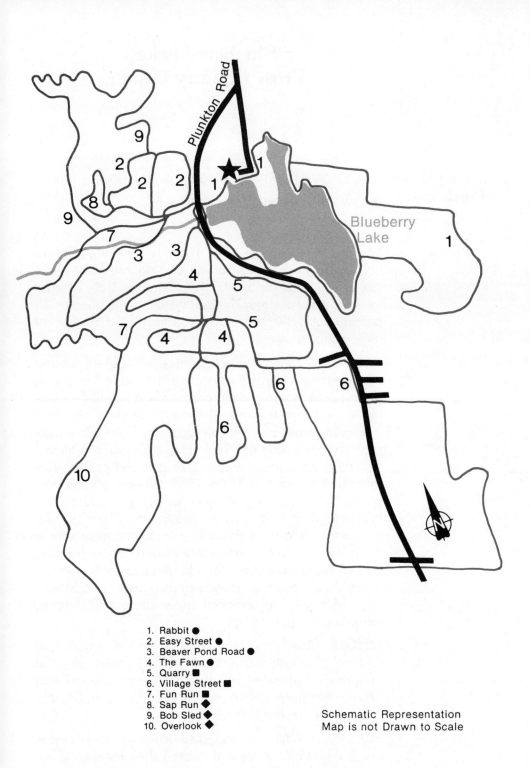

1. Rabbit ●
2. Easy Street ●
3. Beaver Pond Road ●
4. The Fawn ●
5. Quarry ■
6. Village Street ■
7. Fun Run ■
8. Sap Run ◆
9. Bob Sled ◆
10. Overlook ◆

Schematic Representation
Map is not Drawn to Scale

FOOD & LODGING: The ski center offers a minimal selection of hot drinks and trail snacks.

The nearby towns of Warren and Waitsfield have an abundance of inns, bed-and-breakfasts, and restaurants. Two favorites are the Tucker Hill Lodge, offering gourmet food and cozy antique-filled rooms, and the Waitsfield Inn, which has nicely restored colonial architecture and solid food.

Chez Henri is a local institution, where they offer authentic French cuisine and ambience, appropriately priced.

ALPINE FACILITIES IN AREA: Sugarbush, Mad River Glen.

LESSONS: Blueberry Lake is not renowned for its teaching program, although instruction is available in all cross country skiing techniques except telemarking.

SAFETY: There are no regular ski patrols, nor are the trails swept at the close of operations. A parking lot check is made at the end of each day.

CHILDCARE FACILITIES: None.

CONNECTED TO THE CATAMOUNT TRAIL: No.

Gestalt: Blueberry Lake, a homey, friendly, skier-oriented operation with basic amenities, draws a diverse crowd—from Alpine skiers seeking their first Nordic experience to racers in training.

Rabbit is a perfect beginner's loop, with classic Vermont woods to provide protection from the wind, gentle, rolling terrain to provide low-level, low-risk thrills, and a sunny lakeside clearing to cheer the soul.

The Fun Run Loop—featuring nine turns—is one of the most exciting downhill runs in Vermont—a rollicking ride for advanced and intermediate skiers. Fun Run terminates at Easy Street, which allows you to "cool out" with a nice rolling ride back to the cross country ski center.

Blueberry Lake should be commended for its trail map. It's clear and concise and contains all of the information required to make intelligent trail decisions.

Extras: RACES: Blueberry Lake sponsors one or two races each year; call for specific information.

OTHER: A sports facility including tennis and saunas can be found in nearby Sugarbush Valley.

Travel Instructions: FROM BOSTON: Take I-93 north to I-89 north to exit 9 (Route 100)—just beyond Montpelier. Take Route 100B south to Waitsfield Village, make a left in the village through a covered bridge onto Waitsfield Commons Road. Continue until you see signs for Blueberry Lake. The XC center is approximately two miles from the turnoff.

FROM NEW YORK: Take I-91 north to I-89 north and proceed as outlined above.

All of the roads are usually well maintained.

20

Bolton Valley Resorts

BOLTON, VERMONT 05477

For Ski Conditions:

HOURS OF OPERATION: 9:00 A.M. to 5:00 P.M., daily

SNOW PHONE: 802/434-2131

Profile:

TRAILS: Bolton Valley has 33 trails, totaling approximately 75 km. Approximately 45 km of the trails are wilderness trails, including a 23-km trail to Trapp Family Lodge. The number of trails is a little misleading as some of the trails are short. 30 km of the trails are track set, 15 km of which are also groomed for skating. Of the groomed trails, 55 percent are classified as easy, 35 percent more difficult, and 10 percent most difficult. The rest of the system is unpatrolled wilderness.

GROOMING: Unique. Although Bolton Valley uses excellent grooming equipment, they choose to retain a backwoods flavor on their trails by grooming less frequently than most areas and allowing an inch or so of loose powder to build up, rather than hardpacking the trails daily.

RENTALS: Bolton Valley rents a variety of waxless skis and light touring boots, all of which are geared to 75-mm bindings. In addition, they have 20 pairs of back-country, steel-edge, waxable skis, and 15 pairs of Merrell XCD heavy-duty telemark boots. All of which complements their emphasis on a "civilized" back country experience. There are no racing skis (inappropriate for their style of grooming) and no other types of waxable skis available.

FOR WAX LOVERS: A modest selection of wax accessories is available. Waxing is permitted in the wood-stove-heated ski shop, which has a gravel floor and a workbench.

FOOD & LODGING: Although very close to Stowe (about 20 minutes) and the restaurants and hotels that line Route 100, Bolton Valley is an Alpine-skiing destination resort, with the expected variety of condominiums, hotels, inns, bars, and restaurants.

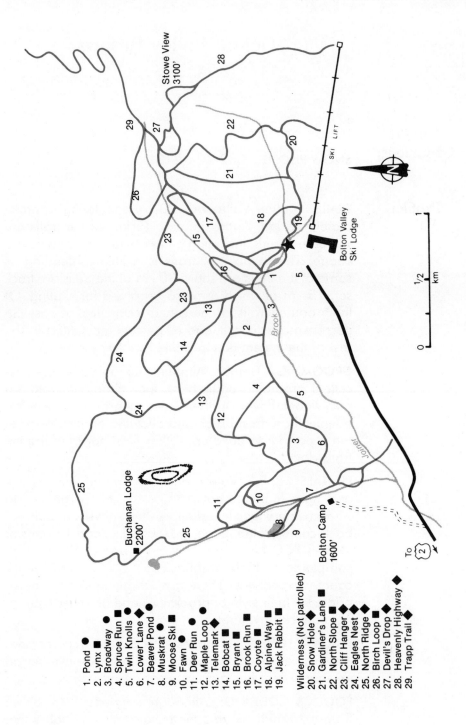

1. Pond ●
2. Lynx ■
3. Broadway ●
4. Spruce Run ●
5. Twin Knolls ●
6. Lower Lane ◆
7. Beaver Pond ◆
8. Muskrat ■
9. Moose Ski ■
10. Fawn ●
11. Deer Run ●
12. Maple Loop ●
13. Telemark ◆
14. Bobcat ■
15. Bryant ■
16. Brook Run ■
17. Coyote ■
18. Alpine Way ■
19. Jack Rabbit ■

Wilderness (Not patrolled)
20. Snow Hole ■
21. Gardiner's Lane ■
22. North Slope ◆
23. Cliff Hanger ◆
24. Eagles Nest ◆
25. North Ridge ■
26. Birch Loop ■
27. Devil's Drop ◆
28. Heavenly Highway ◆
29. Trapp Trail ◆

Bolton Valley has seven restaurants and cafés. The best of the seven, Lindsay's, is also one of the best restaurants in snow country and can be favorably compared with any cosmopolitan establishment. There is also an excellent finger-food lounge, the James Morgan Tavern, overlooking the Alpine ski area.

ALPINE FACILITIES IN AREA: Bolton Valley, Mount Mansfield, Spruce Peak, Smuggler's Notch.

LESSONS: Instruction is available in all methods of cross country skiing. There is a twice weekly telemark clinic on Bolton Mountain, with lessons, ski rental, and lift ticket included in one modest fee.

SAFETY: The trails are patrolled during the day, and all trails are swept at the close of operations on weekends.

CHILDCARE FACILITIES: Yes.

CONNECTED TO THE CATAMOUNT TRAIL: Yes.

Gestalt: Bolton Valley is considered to be part of the Stowe cross country ski system—five cross country ski centers linked by ungroomed trails. Only three of the ski centers in the Stowe area measure up to the standards we set for inclusion in this guidebook; however, of the five centers, Bolton Valley may be the least well known. This could be due to their disregard for the Lycra set, as they cater to backwoods skiers.

Though it sometimes seems like Bolton Valley would be happiest if the clock was turned back 15 years on cross country ski techniques and equipment, their grooming philosophy and trail system provide a refreshing change of pace from the manicured highways of the better known ski centers in the area.

This system is definitely oriented toward intermediate and advanced skiers. If you fall in that category and you enjoy loops that begin and end with a downhill run, try the following: take Broadway, a long, wide, slowish downhill run that is sometimes clogged with beginners, down to the bottom of the system. Begin the loop back to the ski shop on Deer Run, which leads to Maple Loop. When Maple Loop intersects Fox Hollow Loop, take a reading of your energy level. If it's high, go up Fox

Hollow Loop to Bobcat; if it's flagging, go down Fox Hollow Loop to Chickadee. Both Bob Cat and Chickadee lead back to the ski shop via the upper end of Broadway. This entire loop is a series of ups, downs, and flats that never gets boring. There are unexpected, fun turns that are easier to negotiate because of the inch of loose powder intentionally left on the surface.

It is also worth noting that this system sits in a snow pocket ranging from 1,600 to 3,100 feet in elevation and is therefore more likely than most areas to have snow cover during the beginning and end of the season.

Though the Bolton Valley trail map has been improved recently, it still does not provide information on the length of specific trails.

Extras: RACES: None.

OTHER: There is a sports center at Bolton Valley, with tennis, racquetball, saunas, and swimming pool.

Travel Instructions: FROM BOSTON: From I-93 north take I-89 north to exit 10 (Waterbury) and follow Route 2 west seven miles to Bolton Valley.

FROM NEW YORK: Take I-91 north to I-89 north and proceed as outlined above.

The last five miles are a steep ascent up Bolton Mountain that could be difficult to negotiate after a snowstorm, so call ahead for road conditions.

21

Burke Mountain
Cross Country Ski Area

RR1, BOX 62A
EAST BURKE, VERMONT 05832

**For Ski
Conditions:**

HOURS OF OPERATION: 9:00 A.M. to 4:00 P.M., daily

SNOW PHONE: 802/626-8338

Profile:

TRAILS: Burke Mountain has 15 trails totaling approximately 52 km, all of which are groomed and tracked as
needed. Approximately 75 percent of the system is skate
groomed, with tracks set on the right side for classic
skiing. The trail network is classified as 33 percent easy,
30 percent more difficult, and 37 percent most difficult.

GROOMING: Above average. Though Burke Mountain
does not possess state-of-the-art grooming equipment,
they do have a Tucker Snowcat, as well as two snowmobiles. Their biggest grooming asset is Stan Swaim,
the ski center director. With a long history of nordic
skiing management, he grooms all of the trails with
fierce dedication. We recommend that you call ahead if
you suspect icy conditions.

RENTALS: Burke Mountain rents Trak and Fischer waxless skis and a few pairs of waxable skis, all mounted
with 75-mm bindings. The rental boots and poles are
mainly from Alpina and Excel.

FOR WAX LOVERS: A complete supply of wax accessories is available. Waxing is permitted in a heated dome
that doubles as a rest/picnic area.

FOOD & LODGING: A limited selection of snacks and
tasty homemade soups and chilis are available at the ski
center. There are also several inns and bed & breakfast
establishments near Burke Mountain. We recommend
lodging and dining at the Wildflower Inn, which is
charming and immaculate, and features breathtaking
views of the Northeast Kingdom, as well as the best
restaurant in the area. Be sure to ask about the Darling
Mansion, a Newport-style estate, just down the road

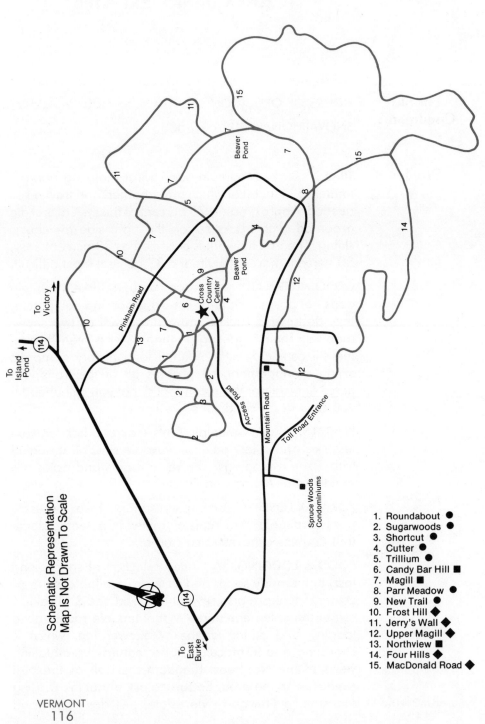

Schematic Representation
Map Is Not Drawn To Scale

To Victory

To Island Pond

114

Pinkham Road

Cross Country Center

Beaver Pond

Beaver Pond

Access Road

Mountain Road

Toll Road Entrance

Spruce Woods Condominiums

To East Burke

114

1. Roundabout ●
2. Sugarwoods ●
3. Shortcut ●
4. Cutter ●
5. Trillium ●
6. Candy Bar Hill ■
7. Magill ■
8. Parr Meadow ●
9. New Trail ●
10. Frost Hill ◆
11. Jerry's Wall ◆
12. Upper Magill ◆
13. Northview ■
14. Four Hills ◆
15. MacDonald Road ◆

from the Inn. If you seek less expensive accommodations, try the Village Inn, a modest bed & breakfast whose proprietor, showing uncommon conscientiousness, once called us to suggest that we cancel our weekend in East Burke because the snow conditions had badly deteriorated.

No one talks about East Burke without mentioning dining at the Old Cutter Inn, a local tradition, which also features spectacular views of the Northeast Kingdom and Willoughby Gap. If your trip to ski country won't be complete without a great breakfast, make a short trip to the Miss Lyndonville Diner in nearby Lyndonville.

ALPINE FACILITIES IN AREA: Burke Mountain.

LESSONS: Instruction is available in all methods of cross country skiing.

SAFETY: The trails are patrolled during the day, but there are no trail sweeps at day's end. The parking lot is monitored for missing skiers. There is also an emergency medical unit at the nearby alpine facility.

CHILDCARE FACILITIES: There is a day-care center at Burke Mountain Alpine Resort.

Gestalt:

Burke Mountain is a bit of a hike from most major cities. Skiers' rewards for willingness to travel are the beauty of the Northeast Kingdom (especially the views of distant Willoughby Gap), a longer and richer snow season, and uncrowded trails.

Burke has an excellent mix of trails for skiers of all levels of ability and conditioning. For intermediate and advanced skiers we recommend the following 6 km loop that has plenty of ups and downs and two beautiful vistas. From the ski center go up Candy Bar Hill (it's steeper than it sounds) to Frost Hill, and enjoy the view at the top. After Frost Hill peaks, it's a curvy, fun, downhill run to Roundabout, which leads back to the ski center. On your ride downhill you will be skiing straight into a classic Vermont mountain vista that is stunning in the glow of late afternoon sun.

If you're seeking challenge and distance, and you're an advanced skier in good condition, try the following 12 km loop. From the ski center take Cutter to Parr

Meadow, both of which are rolling trails that climb toward MacDonald Road. MacDonald Road offers the steepest climb in the trail network (to an elevation of 2,400 feet), as well as the longest and most challenging downhill run. At the end of MacDonald Road, take Magill to Trillium, which leads back to Cutter and the ski center.

The trail map is adequate, but does not present the length of each trail, which we consider an important safety feature.

Extras: RACES: None.

SPECIAL EVENTS: None.

Travel Instructions: FROM BOSTON: Take I-93 to I-91 north and enjoy the views through Franconia Notch. Get off I-91 at Vermont exit 23 and go east on Route 5 through Lyndonville. Then make a right onto Route 114 and go about 5 miles to the center of East Burke. Just past the general store in the center of the village, follow signs (on the right) to the Burke Mountain Alpine Resort. About 200 yards past the entrance to the alpine area, which is on the right, you will find signs pointing toward the nordic area, on the left.

FROM NEW YORK: Take I-91 to Vermont exit 23 and proceed as outlined above.

The final approach to the ski center is a dirt road which can be icy and difficult to negotiate. Call ahead for road conditions.

22

Camel's Hump Nordic Ski Center

R.D. 1, BOX 99, EAST STREET
HUNTINGTON, VERMONT 05462

For Ski Conditions:

HOURS OF OPERATION: 9:00 A.M. to 5:00 P.M. (or dusk), daily

SNOW PHONE: 802/434-2704

Profile:

TRAILS: Camel's Hump has 27 trails, totaling approximately 60 km, of which 35 km are groomed and track set as needed. The number of trails is a little misleading, as some of them are short. Approximately 85 percent of the trails are groomed for skating. Of the groomed trails 20 percent are classified as easy, 70 percent more difficult, and 10 percent most difficult. The rest of the system is unpatrolled wilderness.

GROOMING: Average. Camel's Hump does not use state-of-the-art grooming equipment. The best grooming is done on weekends. Call ahead if you suspect icy conditions.

RENTALS: Camel's Hump does not have a huge quantity of equipment for rent. They have about 20 pairs of Rossignol waxless skis and 10 pairs of Dover waxable skis, all fitted with 75-mm bindings and 30 pairs of assorted 75-mm boots. They also have a few pairs of snowshoes.

FOR WAX LOVERS: A modest selection of wax accessories is available. Waxing is permitted in the wood-stove-heated ski shop, as well as in the recently heated barn.

FOOD & LODGING: Although fairly close to Stowe and the restaurants and hotels that line Route 100, as well as to Burlington (about 20 miles away) and the Mad River Glen resort area, Camel's Hump is pretty remote.

The cross country ski center has two rooms with a shared bath available, bed-and-breakfast style, in a log cabin heated by a massive fieldstone fireplace. Room rates are very reasonable.

The ski center offers hot drinks and snacks (homemade cookies, soups, etc.) by an open fire.

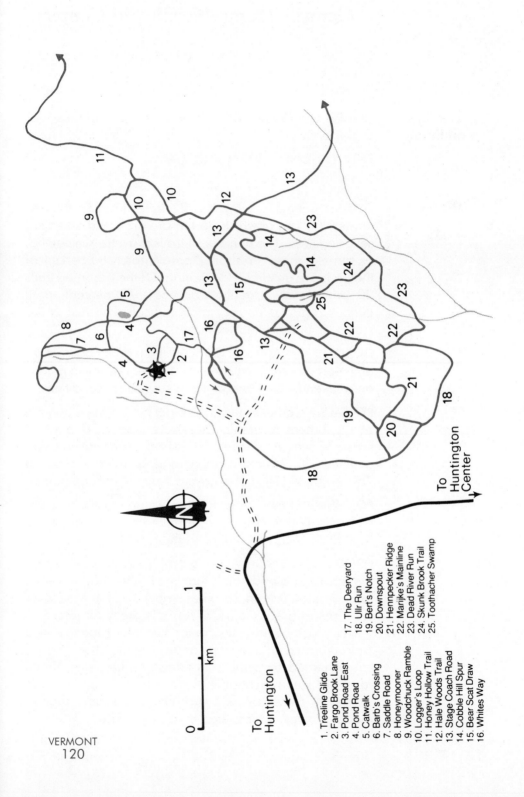

To Huntington

To Huntington Center

km
0   1

1. Treeline Glide
2. Fargo Brook Lane
3. Pond Road East
4. Pond Road
5. Catwalk
6. Barb's Crossing
7. Saddle Road
8. Honeymooner
9. Woodchuck Ramble
10. Loger's Loop
11. Honey Hollow Trail
12. Hale Woods Trail
13. Stage Coach Road
14. Cobble Hill Spur
15. Bear Scat Draw
16. Whites Way
17. The Deeryard
18. Ullr Run
19. Bert's Notch
20. Downspout
21. Hennpecker Ridge
22. Marijke's Mainline
23. Dead River Run
24. Skunk Brook Trail
25. Toothacher Swamp

ALPINE FACILITIES IN AREA: Bolton Valley, Mad River Glen, Mount Mansfield, Spruce Peak, Smuggler's Notch.

LESSONS: Instruction by appointment only is available in all methods of cross country skiing.

SAFETY: There are no regular ski patrols, nor are the trails swept at the close of operations. A parking lot check is made at the end of each day.

CHILDCARE FACILITIES: None.

CONNECTED TO THE CATAMOUNT TRAIL: Yes.

Gestalt: Camel's Hump Nordic Ski Center is spread across 3,000 acres of high, wild, Alpine terrain in a remote area on the western flank of Camel's Hump, Vermont's second highest mountain. The trails rank among the most scenic in New England, with several extraordinary mountain vistas. A feeling of pleasant quiet and isolation dominates.

The cross country ski center facilities are rustic (i.e., outhouse only, though an upscale one), so visitors tend to be hardy types. However, the extensive trail network also attracts expert skiers in search of a solid three- or four-hour ski. This is mostly a knickers-and-gaiters-type place.

Camel's Hump is an important ingredient of the Catamount Trail; information on a marked and skiable 25-km section is available in the lodge. A portion of the Catamount section is Honey Hollow, an incredible trail that climbs to 1,900 feet, then drops 1,500 vertical feet on a nonstop 9-km downhill run to the banks of the Winooski River in Bolton.

For intermediate and advanced skiers who prefer to mix uphills and flats with their downhills, try the 15-km perimeter loop: follow Fargo Brook Lane to Pond Road East, to Berk's Crossing, to Skelly Lane to Echo Woods (which affords a spectacular view of the mountain), then go to Lost Farm Loop and Skywalker to Woodchuck Ramble and Logger's Loop. Ski along Hale Woods Trail to Dead River Run, then Marijke's Mainline to Ullr Run, to Whites Way. From Monarchy Farm Trail, take Gully-whumper back to the cross country ski center.

Extras: RACES: Two or three races are held each year; call for specific information.

SPECIAL EVENTS: Guided night tours with head lamps and moonlight, and special New Year's Eve tour.

Travel Instructions: FROM BOSTON: Take I-93 north to I-89 north, Vermont exit 11 (Richmond). From Richmond follow signs seven miles to Huntington. Pass Jaque's Country Store and bear left at "Y" intersection. Follow signs for two miles to the ski center.

FROM NEW YORK: Follow I-91 north to I-89 north and proceed as outlined above.

The interstate highways are well maintained, but the access road to the XC center is steep and unpaved. Call ahead for road conditions after snowstorms, heavy rains, or during mud season.

23

Craftsbury Nordic Ski Center

BOX 31
CRAFTSBURY COMMON, VERMONT 05827

For Ski Conditions:

HOURS OF OPERATION: 9:00 A.M. to 5:00 P.M., daily

SNOW PHONE: 802/586-2514

Profile:

TRAILS: The Craftsbury trail network is composed of 8 loops that start and finish at the cross country ski center, 13 trail sections, and 3 trails that connect inns (and are part of a guided inn-to-inn tour). They maintain 115 km of ungroomed trails and approximately 65 km of trails that are groomed for both skating and diagonal stride. Of the groomed trails, 20 percent are classified as easy, 50 percent more difficult, and 30 percent most difficult.

GROOMING: Dedicated. Craftsbury is noted for providing skiable loops when most other areas are praying for snow. To begin with, they are located farther north than most cross country ski centers, in a snowy region that is known as the Northeast Kingdom. In addition, they have developed both natural (scooping snow from Hosmer Pond onto ski trails) and artificial (snowmaking equipment) techniques for creating snow-covered trails when nature "ain't" cooperating. Although their grooming equipment is not first class, their grooming people are. As a result, the wide trails are usually in excellent condition. This is definitely a place to consider for early- and late-season skiing.

RENTALS: Craftsbury rents Karhu waxless skis and a few pairs of waxable skis, with either SNS or 75-mm bindings, matched with Salomon or 75-mm boots. A dozen pairs of skate skis are available. They also have two pairs of snowshoes and one pulka (the Scandinavian baby sled).

FOR WAX LOVERS: A complete selection of wax accessories is available. Waxing is permitted in the heated basement of the main dormitory and in the ski shop.

FOOD & LODGING: Although Stowe is in the neighborhood, most people prefer to eat and sleep in Craftsbury

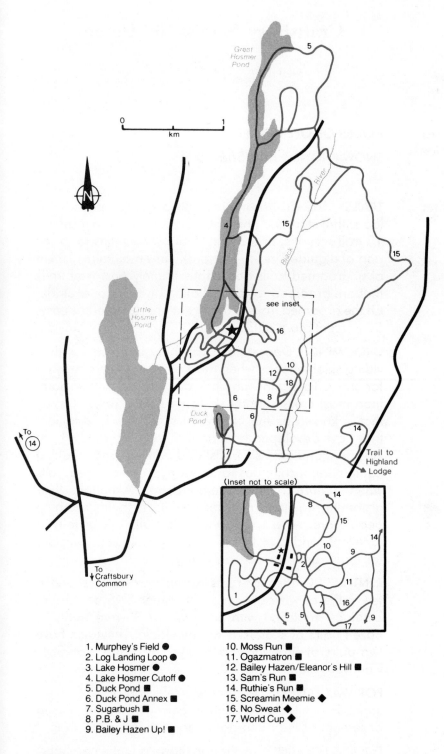

0   1
km

Great
Hosmer
Pond

N

Little
Hosmer
Pond

Black River

5

4

15

15

15

see inset

16

1

12

18

10

6

8

6

10

14

Duck
Pond

7

Trail to
Highland
Lodge

To
(14)

To
Craftsbury
Common

(Inset not to scale)

8

14

15

14

10

9

2

11

1

5

5

7

16

17

9

1. Murphey's Field ●
2. Log Landing Loop ●
3. Lake Hosmer ●
4. Lake Hosmer Cutoff ●
5. Duck Pond ■
6. Duck Pond Annex ■
7. Sugarbush ■
8. P.B. & J ■
9. Bailey Hazen Up! ■

10. Moss Run ■
11. Ogazmatron ■
12. Bailey Hazen/Eleanor's Hill ■
13. Sam's Run ■
14. Ruthie's Run ■
15. Screamin Meemie ◆
16. No Sweat ◆
17. World Cup ◆

Common, where there are two choices: the Inn on the Common, which has Bloomingdale's decor, gourmet food, and prices at the upper end of the scale; or the cross country ski center (a converted prep school), which has a reasonably priced, no-frills selection of dormitory rooms, four apartments, three cottages, and hearty buffets served at 8:00 A.M., 12:30 P.M., and 6:30 P.M.

In addition, the cross country ski center trail network connects six inns in the Craftsbury area. The center will arrange for guided tours suited to your skiing ability and for the transportation of your belongings from one inn to the next.

ALPINE FACILITIES IN AREA: Bolton Valley, Mount Mansfield, Jay Peak, Smuggler's Notch, Burke Mountain.

LESSONS: Instruction is available in all methods of cross country skiing. This place specializes in racing instruction, offering clinics around Thanksgiving and Christmas and in the summer (roller skiing) that feature demonstrations and supervision by some of the top racers in the United States, supplemented by lectures, movies, and video taping. Naturally this expertise spills over into lessons for noncompetitive skiers simply seeking to ski more efficiently.

SAFETY: The trails are patrolled during the day, and all trails are swept at the close of operations.

CHILDCARE FACILITIES: Babysitters are usually available by reservation. There is free childcare during races.

CONNECTED TO THE CATAMOUNT TRAIL: Yes.

Gestalt: Craftsbury seems to have something for everyone and manages to attract a strange mélange of skiers: nationally ranked racers, 70-year-olds from the nearby elder hostel, kids from bus tours. Although the cross country ski center clearly caters to racers, it by no means neglects the average skier. Though the views at Craftsbury are not as spectacular as some areas', people don't come here just for the scenery—they come because of the enthusiastic dedication to the sport evidenced by the management and manifested in the quality of the trails.

A favorite loop for intermediate and advanced skiers is Ruthie's Run, a long (9 km) rolling trail with two major downhills and a lengthy, but gradual, climb through a lovely pine forest. Beginners will enjoy Duck Pond Loop, a 2.5-km trail that is gentle and shielded. Both trails begin and end at the ski center.

Considering management's dedication to the sport, the trail map and trail-marking system are disappointing. The map is somewhat crude and confusing, and you need a magnifying glass to decode some of the information. Because there are so many intersections, the trail-marking system can also be confusing.

Extras:

RACES: Craftsbury hosts many races each year, from December through March. There is usually at least one race in each month of the ski season.

SPECIAL EVENTS: Backcountry ski tours, inn-to-inn skiing, racing clinics, training weekends.

OTHER: If you want to avoid driving, the ski center will arrange (for a fee) to pick you up in Burlington, Montpelier, or Waterbury. Other forms of recreation on the premises include a training room with rowing machines and, believe it or not, a co-ed sauna.

Travel Instructions:

FROM BOSTON: Take I-93 north to I-89 north to I-91 north, exit 21 (St. Johnsbury). Take Route 2 west to West Danville, turn right on Route 15 to Hardwick, where you pick up Route 14 north to Craftsbury Common. About two miles past the common, make a right turn at the sign for the ski center ("Craftsbury Center") and follow the signs.

ALTERNATE ROUTE: Follow I-89 to Montpelier, Vermont, where you pick up Route 14 north to Craftsbury Common.

FROM NEW YORK: Take I-91 north to I-89 north and proceed as outlined above.

The noninterstate highways can be hazardous in foul weather; call ahead for road conditions.

24

Hermitage Cross-Country Touring Center

HANDLE ROAD, P.O. BOX 457
WILMINGTON, VERMONT 05363

For Ski Conditions:

HOURS OF OPERATION: 9:00 A.M. to 4:30 P.M., daily

SNOW PHONE: 802/464-3511 (during operating hours)

Profile:

TRAILS: Hermitage has 15 trails, totaling 44.1 km. Approximately 35 km are groomed and 30 km track set as needed. With the exception of the Ice House Loop, which is double tracked, all trails are groomed to accommodate both classical skiers and skaters. Most of the trails may be skied in two directions. The trail system is classified as 42 percent easy, 14 percent more difficult, and 44 percent most difficult.

GROOMING: Above average. Hermitage is a Pisten Bully short of excellent grooming. In recent years they have acquired a powdermaker and tiller to renovate hard pack and ice.

RENTALS: Hermitage rents a variety of waxless skis with SNS bindings and Salomon boots. They also have a few waxable skis, skating skis, and telemark skis. They have recently added the Salomon Profil system to some of the skating skis.

FOR WAX LOVERS: A complete supply of wax accessories is available. Although they have an unheated waxing shed, waxing is usually permitted in the ski shop, as long as the shop is not too crowded.

FOOD & LODGING: The Hermitage Inn and restaurant has been coasting on its reputation for several years. We have dined there often—with unpredictable results. Sometimes the food is excellent (they raise their own wild game birds and have one of the finest wine cellars in New England) and the service adequate. More often the food is inconsistent and the service is slow. Similarly, the inn is lovely from the outside—oozing New England charm, but

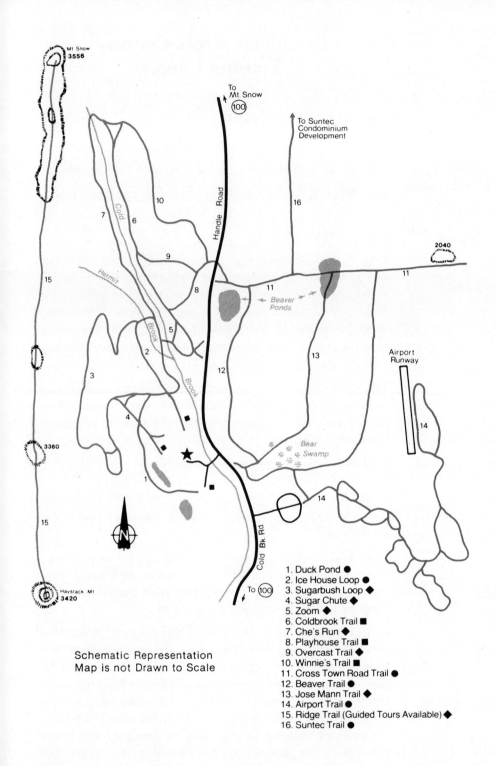

1. Duck Pond ●
2. Ice House Loop ●
3. Sugarbush Loop ◆
4. Sugar Chute ◆
5. Zoom ◆
6. Coldbrook Trail ■
7. Che's Run ◆
8. Playhouse Trail ■
9. Overcast Trail ◆
10. Winnie's Trail ■
11. Cross Town Road Trail ●
12. Beaver Trail ●
13. Jose Mann Trail ◆
14. Airport Trail ●
15. Ridge Trail (Guided Tours Available) ◆
16. Suntec Trail ●

Schematic Representation
Map is not Drawn to Scale

some of the parts (beds, plumbing) may not be as charming as the whole. The availability of rooms is limited, so making reservations well in advance is recommended.

There are many other lodging and dining establishments in the area.

ALPINE FACILITIES IN AREA: Mount Snow and Haystack Mountain.

LESSONS: Instruction is available in all methods of cross country skiing. With the immediate accessibility of excellent Alpine skiing, Hermitage specializes in telemark and Norpine lessons.

SAFETY: Hermitage conducts regular patrols and end-of-the-day trail sweeps on weekends only.

CHILDCARE FACILITIES: None.

CONNECTED TO THE CATAMOUNT TRAIL: Yes.

Gestalt: Skiing Hermitage can be one of the most delightful cross country experiences in New England. The first delight encountered on all of the trails that lead up into the mountains is the quacking and chirping of the beautiful game birds penned near Duck Pond Trail. A fun, before-lunch loop for intermediate and advanced skiers begins with Ice House Loop, which connects via a picturesque bridge with Coldbrook Trail. Proceed up Coldbrook Trail to the junction with Che's Run and Winnie's Run. The more advanced skier may wish to circle back down Che's Run and connect with Sugarbush Loop via a short ski on the Ice House Loop, while those desiring more moderate downhill thrills may prefer the more gentle, but still satisfying, downhill of Winnie's Run. Cross over Handle Road and take Cross Town Road Trail to either Jose Mann Trail or Powerline. The Airport Trail, which we found boring before we learned how to skate, is now a favorite with skaters for the same factors that made it boring to classic skiers—generous width and consistent terrain.

Probably the most interesting, challenging, and breathtaking trail at Hermitage is Ridge Trail, which runs along the ridge between Haystack and Mount Snow peaks. The trail map states, "Not meant for the faint at heart. Great views of Massachusetts, New Hampshire, and Vermont, with the highest elevation at 3,556 feet. Best skied with Norpine equipment." This trail is not always open, however, since it requires a lot of snow to be skiable.

Be aware that the most difficult trails are generally the last to be groomed, so call ahead and request conditions for specific trails before heading to Hermitage.

Extras:

RACES: Races at Hermitage include the Mount Snow Ridge Run (always the first Sunday in February).

Each year Hermitage offers a different version of the St. Patrick's Day Race, which barely deserves the name "race," though all contestants are timed. The event includes an obstacle course and ski shenanigans. Those who have ideas about winning are sure to lose.

SPECIAL EVENTS: A variety of clinics and guided Ridge Trail tours.

OTHER: Saunas and heated swimming pools are available in the area.

Travel Instructions:

FROM BOSTON: Take Route 2 west to I-91 north, exit in Brattleboro on Route 9 west, and take Route 100 north; look for signs to Hermitage.

FROM NEW YORK: From I-91 north follow the route outlined above.

All roads are usually well maintained.

25

Highland Lodge

CASPIAN LAKE
GREENSBORO, VERMONT 05841

For Ski Conditions:

HOURS OF OPERATION: 9:00 A.M. to 4:00 P.M., daily

SNOW PHONE: 802/533-2647

Profile:

TRAILS: Highland Lodge has 7 interconnected loops, totaling approximately 65 km, all of which are rolled; 30 km are track set as needed. Skating is not encouraged. The trail system is classified as 33 percent easy and 67 percent more difficult; none are designated most difficult.

GROOMING: Average. Highland Lodge has good grooming equipment, but it is not state of the art. They can generally handle marginal conditions, unless one of the ingredients is wind, and then the openness of the trails negates most grooming efforts and makes skiing more difficult.

RENTALS: Highland Lodge rents Trak and Karhu waxless skis and Rossignol waxable skis, with 75-mm bindings and Merrell 75-mm boots. They also have four pairs of snowshoes.

FOR WAX LOVERS: A complete selection of wax accessories is available. Waxing is permitted in the heated ski shop.

FOOD & LODGING: You found the cross country ski center, now try the accommodations and food at the Highland Lodge. The Lodge presents itself as a family refuge from the tensions of modern life. They can accommodate 60 peace seekers.

All of the food at the lodge is homemade, of high-quality ingredients, cooked and served with pride.

ALPINE FACILITIES IN AREA: None.

LESSONS: Instruction is available in all traditional methods of cross country skiing—nothing fancy, no skating or telemarking, just basic diagonal stride.

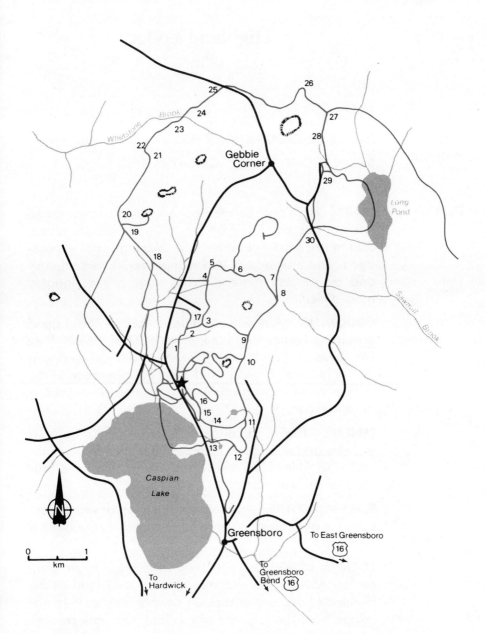

Numbers correspond to signposts

SAFETY: The trails are not patrolled during the day, nor are the trails swept at the close of operations. All skiers are asked to register before embarking and sign out upon completion of their ski.

CHILDCARE FACILITIES: With advance notice, baby-sitting services can be arranged.

CONNECTED TO THE CATAMOUNT TRAIL: No.

Gestalt: We have included Highland Lodge in this guidebook for aesthetic reasons—the trails are gorgeous. You ski through fields and valleys, delineated by rows of trees and sugar bushes, with stunning views over open pasturelands of Mount Mansfield (Vermont's highest peak) to the west, Burke Mountain to the east, the Lowell Mountain Range to the north, and Caspian Lake below. There is no finer place for spring skiing and picnics.

You won't find Lycra racing suits here, only good, steady skiers. Highland Lodge attracts families and couples who ski to lose themselves in nature, stop to look at animal tracks, and admire the vistas. The patrons seem to be low-key, self-directed, and relaxed.

A favorite trail of beginners and intermediates is the Barr Hill Loop (checkpoints 1-10). It's a solid hour-plus ski for sub-experts, though additional time is generally consumed by those stopping to absorb the scenic eyeful. The trail winds around the shoulder of a hill and presents a panorama of much of northern Vermont. To extend the tour, simply add one of the adjoining loops.

Extras: **RACES:** None.

SPECIAL EVENTS: Monthly moonlight tours.

OTHER: Sledding for kids near the ski shop.

Travel Instructions: **FROM BOSTON:** From I-93 north take I-89 north to I-91 north, exit 21 (St. Johnsbury). Take Route 2 west to West Danville, turn right on Route 15 to Hardwick, a few miles before Hardwick turn right on Route 16 and go two miles to East Hardwick. In East Hardwick turn left and follow signs four miles to Greensboro.

FROM NEW YORK: Take I-91 north and proceed as outlined above.

The non-interstate highways can present hazardous driving in foul weather; call ahead for road conditions.

26

Mount Mansfield Ski Touring Center

STOWE, VERMONT 05672

For Ski Conditions:

HOURS OF OPERATION: 9:00 A.M. to 4:00 P.M., daily

SNOW PHONE: 802/253-7311

Profile:

TRAILS: Mount Mansfield has 19 trails, totaling approximately 50 km. The system includes 26 km of unpatrolled wilderness trails, some of which connect to Trapp Family Lodge; 24 km are groomed and double-track set as needed. Skating is permitted on all trails. Of the groomed trails, 30 percent are classified as easy, 37 percent more difficult, and 33 percent most difficult.

GROOMING: Above average. Though Mount Mansfield's grooming equipment is far from primitive, it is not state of the art. They do possess a powder maker for grooming during frozen conditions, but if the Mount Mansfield Corporation (which also manages the Alpine facility and related real estate developments) wants to match the grooming of its more renowned Austrian neighbor (Trapp), they must allocate some funds for topflight grooming equipment.

RENTALS: Mount Mansfield rents Rossignol waxless skis and has an assortment of waxable skis, all of which are mounted with either Salomon (SNS) or 75-mm bindings. They rent Salomon and 75-mm boots. There are no racing skis available.

FOR WAX LOVERS: A complete selection of wax accessories is available. Waxing is permitted in the wood-stove-heated ski shop.

FOOD & LODGING: Snacks are sold in the ski shop. However, this ski center sits smack in the middle of Stowe, which offers the largest variety of restaurants, inns, and hotels of any ski area in Vermont.

Two reasonably priced favorites are the Stow Away and the Timberholme Inn. The Stow Away is a funky inn with a terrific Mexican restaurant (the best Mexican food we've had north of New York City), and the joint is

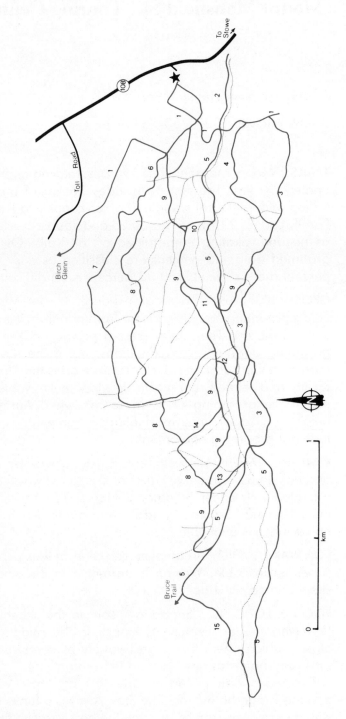

Legend:
1. Stowe Derby Trail
2. Ranch Road
3. Ranch Valley Cruise
4. River View
5. Burt Trail
6. Townhouse Trail
7. The Double Bit
8. Peavey Trail
9. Timber Lane
10. Cross Cut 1
11. Cross Cut 2
12. Cross Cut 3
13. Cross Cut 4
14. The Wedge
15. Bear Run

108

To Stowe

Toll Road

Birch Glenn

Bruce Trail

N

km

0 1

always jumpin'. By contrast, the Timberholme Inn is a quiet, inexpensive place to bed down. The core of the inn is a charming living-dining area, featuring a massive stone fireplace, in front of which you can breakfast on eggs laid by Timberholme's chickens. The rooms are arranged dormitory style and serviced by shared men's and women's bathrooms. They have recently added several rooms with private baths.

ALPINE FACILITIES IN AREA: Mount Mansfield, Spruce Peak, Smuggler's Notch, Bolton Valley.

LESSONS: Instruction is available in all methods of cross country skiing. In addition, there is an excellent area for telemark skiing; lift service is available.

SAFETY: The trails are patrolled during the day, and all trails are swept at the close of operations.

CHILDCARE FACILITIES: Yes.

CONNECTED TO THE CATAMOUNT TRAIL: Yes.

Gestalt: Mount Mansfield is part of the Stowe cross country ski network—five cross country ski centers linked by ungroomed trails, only three of which measure up to the standards we set for inclusion in this guidebook. Of the top three Stowe ski centers, Mount Mansfield sits in the middle of the road: it caters more to the backwoods skiers than Trapp Family Lodge and attracts more of the Lycra set than Bolton Valley.

There is a variety of terrain at Mount Mansfield, but no long, flat stretches. Even the 7-km beginner loop is rolling. During icy conditions, beginners without an adequate snowplow may spend more time on their rear ends than on their skis.

Intermediate and advanced skiers will enjoy the following loop, which is constantly changing and never boring: from the ski shop take Timber Lane to Bruce Trail and continue up to Bear Run. Though this 4-km ski is predominantly uphill, it is rolling, which lightens the load. At the "T" intersection of Bruce Trail and Bear Run you can turn either right or left to a series of delightful downhill runs; however, we prefer turning left. Take Bear Run to the Burt Trail and cruise back to the ski shop. This loop is approximately 9 km.

If you are an advanced skier who enjoys wilderness skiing, you should try the well-maintained, but un-groomed, trails that separate the Mount Mansfield Touring Center from the Trapp Family Lodge. The shortest trail with the best potential resting spot is the 4-km Ranch Camp Trail, which is accessible from the ski shop via two groomed trails, Burt Trail (2.5 km) or Ranch Valley Cruise (3 km). The Ranch Camp Trail runs directly into Haul Road, a groomed trail in the Trapp system that offers beautiful vistas of Mount Mansfield and leads directly to the Trapp ski cabin, where you can get hot soup and beverages. After resting, you can either accept the challenge of returning to the Mount Mansfield head-quarters via wilderness trails or, if weary, ski down the groomed trails of the Trapp system (see recommendations on page 155) and arrange for transportation back to the point of origin.

Mount Mansfield offers a beautiful, clear, Alpine-style trail map with one major flaw: the degree of difficulty of each trail is not presented.

Extras: **RACES:** Winter Carnival Race in January.

Travel Instructions: **FROM BOSTON:** Follow I-93 north to I-89 north, exit 10 (Waterbury). Take Route 100 north to the center of Stowe and turn left on Route 108 (Mountain Road); the ski center is about five miles on the left.

FROM NEW YORK: Take I-91 north to I-89 north and proceed as outlined above.

The roads to Stowe are generally well maintained and plowed during snowstorms.

Mountain Top
Cross Country Ski Resort

MOUNTAIN TOP ROAD
CHITTENDEN, VERMONT 05737

For Ski Conditions:

HOURS OF OPERATION: 9:00 A.M. to 5:00 P.M., daily

SNOW PHONE: 802/483-6089 (during operating hours)
800/445-2100 (after hours)

Profile:

TRAILS: Mountain Top has 28 trails, totaling 110 km, including 40 km of wilderness trails that are part of the Catamount Trail. Approximately 35 km are groomed and double-track set daily. At any given time, there are generally 50 km groomed. All of the trails have been designed to accommodate skating, and may be skied in two directions. The trail system is classified as 17 percent easy, 36 percent more difficult, and 47 percent most difficult.

GROOMING: Excellent. Mountain Top uses state-of-the-art grooming equipment. We enjoyed excellent skiing at Mountain Top on a day when another large nearby system selected for testing was one massive, solid block of ice. In addition, Mountain Top is one of the few areas to have purchased snowmaking equipment, which they use over a 2½ km loop during periods of lean snow cover.

RENTALS: Mountain Top rents Rossignol waxless skis, with SNS bindings, Salomon boots, and Exel poles. They also rent skating and telemark skis, snowshoes, ice skates, luge sleds, and toboggans.

FOR WAX LOVERS: A complete supply of wax accessories is available. A well equipped waxing area is provided in the rental shop.

FOOD & LODGING: A small, but well-considered, selection of snacks is available in the skiing center. More substantial fare and comfort is provided by the Mountain Top Inn, which sits in the middle of the trail network, with gorgeous views of Chittenden Reservoir and the surrounding mountains. Mountain Top is one of the best run inns in Snow Country. In addition, the XC center is

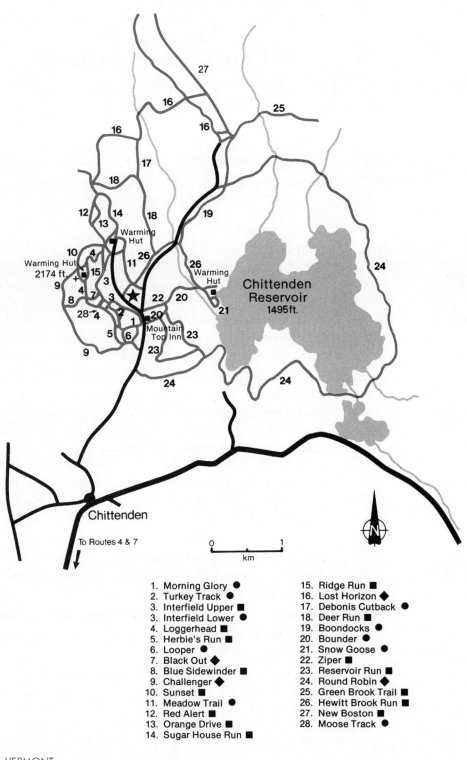

27

16

25

16

16

17

16

18

19

12 14

13

18

Warming
Hut

10   4

Warming Hut
2174 ft.   15   11   26

9   +   4

4   3   26
8   7   Warming
3   Hut

28 4   2   Chittenden
5   1   Reservoir
9   6   1495 ft.

24

22   20

20

Mountain   23
Top Inn
23

24

24

21

Chittenden

To Routes 4 & 7

0   1
km

N

1. Morning Glory ●
2. Turkey Track ●
3. Interfield Upper ■
3. Interfield Lower ●
4. Loggerhead ■
5. Herbie's Run ■
6. Looper ●
7. Black Out ◆
8. Blue Sidewinder ■
9. Challenger ◆
10. Sunset ■
11. Meadow Trail ●
12. Red Alert ■
13. Orange Drive ■
14. Sugar House Run ■

15. Ridge Run ■
16. Lost Horizon ◆
17. Debonis Cutback ●
18. Deer Run ■
19. Boondocks ●
20. Bounder ●
21. Snow Goose ●
22. Ziper ■
23. Reservoir Run ■
24. Round Robin ◆
25. Green Brook Trail ■
26. Hewitt Brook Run ■
27. New Boston ■
28. Moose Track ●

only a half-hour drive from Killington, and the road between Alpine and Nordic skiing is packed with hotels and restaurants.

ALPINE FACILITIES IN AREA: Killington, Pico Peak.

LESSONS: How would you like some tips from two of the greatest skiers in American nordic history? The Mountain Top instruction team is supervised by Mike Gallagher, the former Olympic competitor and coach, who was recently inducted into the skiing hall of fame. If that's not impressive enough, would you like a clinic with Bill Koch? Mr. Koch, the former Olympic medalist who is credited with popularizing the skating technique, conducts several clinics at Mountain Top each year for skiers of all levels of ability. Needless to say, instruction is available in all methods of cross country skiing.

SAFETY: Although the trails are not swept at the end of the day, they are patrolled during operating hours. Skiers are asked to register before embarking on the trails.

CHILDCARE FACILITIES: Babysitters are available on request. Call well in advance.

CONNECTED TO THE CATAMOUNT TRAIL: Yes.

Gestalt: Mountain Top is one of the top ten XC centers in New England. This trail system has everything we looked for in a great ski area: challenging terrain, intelligently cut trails, excellent grooming, beauty and charm, and dedicated management.

There are three warming huts scattered about the system that some skiers may want to use as lunch destinations. Though the Sugar House is heated, the other two huts are unattended; it is the skiers' responsibility to prepare a fire. Two of the huts are readily accessible to beginners via easy trails; the third hut is at the top of the system and can be reached only by a prolonged, steep climb.

Although beginning skiers will find enough kilometers to keep them busy, Mountain Top clearly favors intermediate and advanced skiers. A challenging intermediate ski for a first time at Mountain Top begins with a steep climb up Loggerhead to the warming hut. Take a brief pause to catch your breath, then get ready for what is mostly a wonderful roller-coaster ride downhill to the ski center. Begin the descent by continuing on Loggerhead to Red Alert. Red Alert provides an extraordinary view of Chittenden Reservoir and the surrounding mountains, one of the best vistas in New England. Take Red Alert to Lost Horizon until it intersects Deer Run. At this intersection, take stock of your stamina and choose either the delightful, rolling terrain of Deer Run, which terminates within a kilometer of the ski center, or the much longer Lost Horizon, which terminates farther down the valley and requires a long, steady (perhaps boring) climb to reach the ski center.

Mountain Top should be regarded as a mecca for the Lycra skating set. Although skating was initially restricted to certain trails, all trails have been widened to a minimum of 12 feet, and now there are no restrictions on skating.

It is also worthwhile to note that Mountain Top has one of the best maps and trail-marking systems in New England.

Extras: RACES: None.

OTHER: Horse-drawn sleigh rides, ice-skating, and tobogganing are available.

Travel Instructions: FROM BOSTON: Take I-93 north to I-89 north, exit 1. Follow Route 4 west past Woodstock, Killington, and Pico. Near Mendon look for signs on the right to Chittenden and Mountain Top Inn. Turn right on Meadowlake Drive and follow the signs to Chittenden and the Mountain Top Inn.

FROM NEW YORK: Follow I-87 north to Route 4 east; take Route 4 east to Rutland and Route 7. Follow Route 7 north (past a power station on the left) to Chittenden Road (a small road with a country store on the left). Follow the signs on Chittenden Road to Chittenden and the Mountain Top Inn.

Routes 4 and 7 are usually well maintained during snowstorms; once you leave the state highways, however, you must have a vehicle that can handle snow covered roads. This is especially true of the final mile to the inn (they don't call it "Mountain Top" for nothing). Call ahead for road conditions.

28

Ole's Cross Country

AIRPORT ROAD
WARREN, VERMONT 05674

For Ski Conditions:

HOURS OF OPERATION: 9:00 A.M. to 5:00 P.M., daily

SNOW PHONE: 802/496-3430

Profile:

TRAILS: Ole's has 10 trails, totaling approximately 72 km, of which 54 km are groomed and track set as needed. None of the trails are groomed for skating. Of the groomed trails, 28 percent are classified as easy, 32 percent more difficult, and 40 percent most difficult.

GROOMING: Above average. Though Ole's does not use state-of-the-art grooming equipment, they insist on top-quality grooming. The main trail loops are usually in good condition, but they use homemade equipment to grind up frozen snow, so this may be a marginal place to ski on a marginal day.

RENTALS: Ole's rents about 40 pairs of waxless skis and 40 pairs of waxable skis sporting the logos of a variety of manufacturers. Most of the bindings are 75 mm matched with Alfa boots. They also have a few pairs of racing skis.

FOR WAX LOVERS: A complete selection of wax accessories is available. There is a heated waxing area.

FOOD & LODGING: Ole's offers skiers' lunches (soups, sandwiches, etc.) at the ski center.

Ole's is only two miles from the Blueberry Lake Cross Country Center, so if the following recommendations strike a familiar note, it's because you've heard this tune before. The nearby towns of Warren and Waitsfield have numerous inns, bed-and-breakfasts, and restaurants. The Tucker Hill Lodge offers gourmet food and cozy antique-filled rooms, and the Waitsfield Inn features nicely restored colonial architecture and solid food.

Chez Henri is a local institution that offers authentic French cuisine and ambience at appropriate prices.

ALPINE FACILITIES IN AREA: Sugarbush, Mad River Glen.

All trails beginner to intermediate difficulty

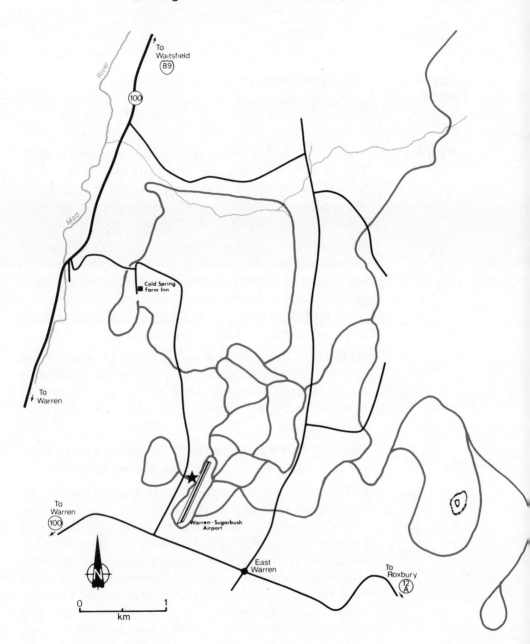

To Waitsfield
89

100

River

Mad

Cold Spring
Farm Inn

To Warren

To Warren
100

Warren - Sugarbush
Airport

N

0   1
km

East Warren

To Roxbury
12
A

LESSONS: Instruction is available in all methods of cross country skiing except for telemarking.

SAFETY: There are no regular ski patrols, nor are the trails swept at the close of operations. A parking lot check is made at the end of each day.

CHILDCARE FACILITIES: None.

CONNECTED TO THE CATAMOUNT TRAIL: No.

Gestalt:

Ole's sits on a high plateau surrounded by mountain ridges. On a sunny day the open terrain affords spectacular views of the mountains. On a windy, nasty day, you will want to seek the protection of the woods. The ski shop is located in the architecturally delightful control tower of the Warren-Sugarbush airport, which is closed during the winter.

Ole Mosesen, the Norwegian proprietor, has been running this one-man operation since 1971, and the place definitely bears his imprimatur. His ski center attracts both beginners and seasoned experts.

There are a number of trails that are good for beginners with mild uphills and easy descents with long runouts.

A favorite trail of intermediate and advanced skiers is the 10-km Holly King Trail. This is a two- to three-hour ski that includes a long climb up open fields, a jog across a long trail winding through woods and fields, and a terrific, long downhill run.

Extras:

RACES: There is at least one race each year; call for specific information.

SPECIAL EVENTS: There are waxing clinics every Wednesday at 4:00 P.M. and occasional moonlight tours.

OTHER: A sports facility including tennis and saunas can be found in nearby Sugarbush Valley.

Travel Instructions:

OLE'S CROSS COUNTRY
145

FROM BOSTON: From I-93 north take I-89 north to exit 9 (Route 100). Take Route 100B south to Waitsfield Village, make a left in the village through a covered bridge, and proceed seven miles to Roxbury Mountain Road. Make a right turn at the crossroad and continue one-half mile to Airport Road. Turn right; the XC center is at the airport.

ALTERNATE ROUTE: If the weather is good and the roads are clear, a quicker and more scenic route begins at I-89, exit 3. Take Route 107 south to Route 100, go north on Route 100 to Warren, turn right (east) on Brook Road. Go two miles and turn left, then left again at Roxbury Mountain Road, continue one-half mile to Airport Road, and turn right.

FROM NEW YORK: Take I-91 north to I-89 north and proceed as outlined above.

All of the roads are well maintained.

29

Prospect Mountain
Ski Touring Center

HCR 65 BOX 760
WOODFORD, VERMONT 05201

For Ski Conditions:

HOURS OF OPERATION: 9:00 A.M. to dusk, daily

SNOW PHONE: 802/442-2575

Profile:

TRAILS: Prospect Mountain has 16 trails totaling approximately 35 km, all of which are groomed and tracked as needed. All of the trails are exceptionally wide (15–20 feet) and skate groomed, with tracks set on the right side for classic skiing. In addition, before the snow flies a blanket of grass (which is maintained and mowed) covers all of the trails, allowing Prospect to provide skiing with just six inches of snow. The trail network is classified as 35 percent easy, 30 percent more difficult, and 35 percent most difficult.

GROOMING: Excellent. Prospect Mountain has state-of-the-art grooming equipment and knows how to use it. We skied Prospect the day after a soaking rain followed by a quick freeze at 3:00 A.M. The conditions in their parking lot were so treacherous that we were almost afraid to try skiing, but the ski trails were groomed to perfection. This is a great place to call when you suspect icy conditions at other ski areas.

RENTALS: Prospect Mountain rents Trak waxless skis, boots, and poles. They also have a few pairs of skating skis, but no kick-waxable skis. Their supply of rental equipment is limited, so call ahead and make sure they have enough rentals to fill your needs.

FOR WAX LOVERS: A complete supply of wax accessories is available. Waxing is permitted in the heated building where trail tickets are sold. A work bench and electrical outlets are provided.

FOOD & LODGING: Right at the base lodge of the ski center is Buck's Tavern, a no-frills restaurant that serves tasty soups and sandwiches during the day and meals

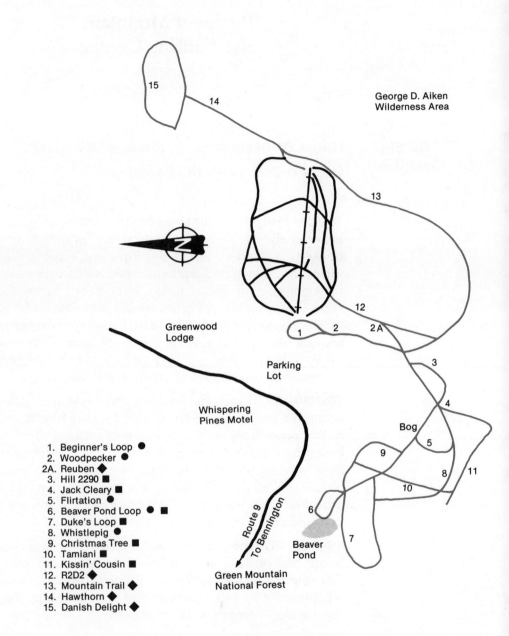

George D. Aiken
Wilderness Area

15

14

13

N

12

Greenwood
Lodge

1 2 2A

Parking
Lot

3

4

Whispering
Pines Motel

Bog

5

9

8 11

1. Beginner's Loop ●
2. Woodpecker ●
2A. Reuben ◆
3. Hill 2290 ■
4. Jack Cleary ■
5. Flirtation ●
6. Beaver Pond Loop ● ■
7. Duke's Loop ■
8. Whistlepig ●
9. Christmas Tree ■
10. Tamiani ■
11. Kissin' Cousin ■
12. R2D2 ◆
13. Mountain Trail ◆
14. Hawthorn ◆
15. Danish Delight ◆

10

6

7

Beaver
Pond

Route 9
To Bennington

Green Mountain
National Forest

(with entertainment) during the evening. Buck's Tavern offers a view of both alpine and cross country activities.

Prospect Mountain sits right in between Bennington and Wilmington, both of which feature a plethora of inns, bed-and-breakfasts, and dining establishments.

ALPINE FACILITIES IN AREA: Prospect Mountain, Haystack, Mount Snow.

LESSONS: Instruction is available in all methods of cross country skiing. This is an ideal place to learn skating and telemarking.

SAFETY: The trails are swept at the end of each day.

CHILDCARE FACILITIES: None.

Gestalt: Prospect Mountain is both an alpine and cross country facility operating out of the same group of buildings. It is also the only ski area in New England where alpine skiing takes a back seat to cross country skiing.

Prospect is arguably the best area in New England to practice skating. Unlike most of the areas described in this book, the easy and more difficult trails at Prospect are relatively flat, so one can concentrate on technique rather than conditioning and stamina. The drawback to great skating trails is their width, which makes them feel more like roads than trails through the woods.

The other drawback at Prospect is that they don't have enough kilometers of trails to keep a good skier busy for more than a day. In fact, an advanced skier could ski the whole system in a few hours. However, we have been assured that the new owners of Prospect have plans to activate some old trails and build new ones.

If you're looking for downhill thrills, ski all of the most difficult trails. Either take the easy way to the top of Prospect Mountain (the alpine ski lift) or earn your thrills by skiing up Mountain Trail to Hawthorn and Danish Delight, returning to the base lodge on the same trails.

For a great rolling ski, what I like to call cruise control, try the perimeter loop of easy and more difficult trails. From the base lodge take Woodpecker to Hill 2290 to Jack Cleary to Kissin' Cousin, to Tamiami, left on Whistlepig, left on Duke's Loop, left on Beaver Pond Loop, to

Christmas Tree, to Beaver Pond, and back to the base lodge on Woodpecker.

It is also worth noting that to ski the easy and more difficult trails you must begin with a modest climb from the base lodge. If you don't like the idea of starting your ski out of breath, management has provided a tow rope to get you over the first hump.

The trail map is adequate, but does not present the length of each trail, which we consider an important safety feature.

Extras: RACES: The new owners of Prospect have not had time to plan a permanent race schedule. Nevertheless, in their first year of operation they hosted many collegiate races and some citizen races. Call for information.

SPECIAL EVENTS: None.

Travel Instructions: FROM BOSTON: Take Massachusetts Route 2 to Interstate 91. Go north on 91 and exit at Vermont Route 9 near Brattleboro. Go west on Route 9. Prospect Mountain is on Route 9 between Wilmington and Bennington.

FROM NEW YORK: Take I-91 to Vermont and proceed as outlined above.

All roads are well maintained.

30

Trapp Family Lodge
Cross Country Touring Center

STOWE, VERMONT 05672

For Ski Conditions:

HOURS OF OPERATION: 9:00 A.M. to 5:00 P.M., daily

SNOW PHONE: 802/253-8511

Profile:

TRAILS: Trapps' has 19 trails, totaling approximately 100 km, of which 60 km are groomed and double-track set daily. Most of the groomed trails have been widened to accommodate both skating and diagonal stride. The remaining 40 km of ungroomed and unpatrolled trails connect Trapps' with the Bolton Valley and Mount Mansfield cross country centers. Of the groomed trails, 15 percent are classified as easy, 45 percent more difficult, and 40 percent most difficult.

GROOMING: Excellent. Trapps' uses state-of-the-art grooming equipment. During icy conditions, the easy trails in the immediate vicinity of the ski shop, which are not protected from the wind, can become impenetrable boiler plate; however, if you have the skills to get past Picnic Knoll there are usually plenty of skiable tracks.

RENTALS: Trapps' offers a huge inventory of rental equipment: Fischer Crown waxless skis and an assortment of waxable skis, all of which are mounted with either Salomon (SNS) or 75-mm bindings, matched by Salomon or 75-mm boots. They also rent Fischer, Blizzard, and Kneissl racing skis and have demonstration equipment available in all skis and poles they sell.

FOR WAX LOVERS: A complete selection of wax accessories is available. Below the retail ski shop, near the rental area, they have provided an excellent waxing area (heated, of course) with ski braces, workbenches, and electrical outlets.

FOOD & LODGING: Although the Trapp complex overlooks Stowe, which offers the largest variety of restaurants, inns, and hotels of any ski area in Vermont, we

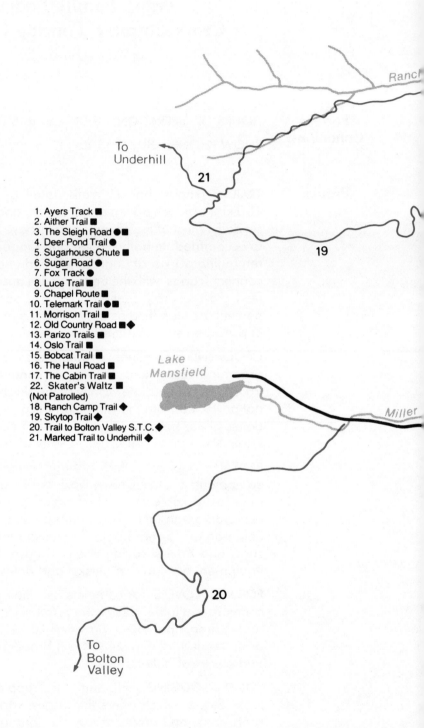

Ranch

To
Underhill

21

19

1. Ayers Track ■
2. Aither Trail ■
3. The Sleigh Road ●■
4. Deer Pond Trail ●
5. Sugarhouse Chute ■
6. Sugar Road ●
7. Fox Track ●
8. Luce Trail ■
9. Chapel Route ■
10. Telemark Trail ●■
11. Morrison Trail ■
12. Old Country Road ■◆
13. Parizo Trails ■
14. Oslo Trail ■
15. Bobcat Trail ■
16. The Haul Road ■
17. The Cabin Trail ■
22. Skater's Waltz ■
(Not Patrolled)
18. Ranch Camp Trail ◆
19. Skytop Trail ◆
20. Trail to Bolton Valley S.T.C. ◆
21. Marked Trail to Underhill ◆

Lake
Mansfield

Miller

20

To
Bolton
Valley

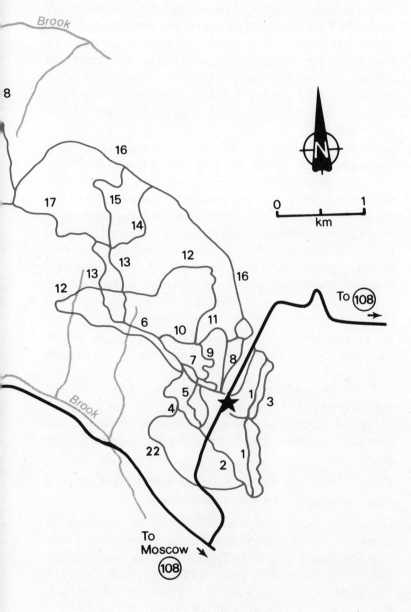

cannot discuss this cross country ski center without considering the Trapp Family Lodge.

Even though a disastrous fire destroyed the main lodge in 1980 (it has since been rebuilt), Trapps' is still the only New England hostelry we have visited that opted for traditional European mountain architecture and succeeded. An atmosphere of old world charm and grace pervades this monument to the Trapp family, and the flavor of the place is further enhanced by its setting. Hollywood couldn't fantasize a better landscape for a ski lodge.

Food at Trapps' is offered in several imaginative packages. Basic hot drinks and snacks are available at the cross country ski center, where they can be consumed in front of a massive roaring fire while you view the beautiful Green Mountains and the steady stream of skiers departing on and returning from the trails. Hearty homemade soup and sandwiches are served at Slayton Pasture Cabin, which is perched near the top of the trail network. More civilized fare is provided in the Austrian Tea Room and Bar, a Tyrolean edifice featuring full meals, pastries, drinks, and grand vistas. The final step up in elegance is offered at the main lodge, where Austrian cuisine is the specialty. You weren't expecting chop suey?

That's the good news; the bad news is that this is a very popular resort, so early reservations are a must.

For information on other possibilities in Stowe, see comments on the Mount Mansfield Ski Touring Center (page 135).

ALPINE FACILITIES IN AREA: Mount Mansfield, Spruce Peak, Smuggler's Notch, Bolton Volley.

LESSONS: Instruction is available in all methods of cross country skiing. Private lessons include video taping. The teaching staff at Trapps' includes some of the most knowledgeable instructors and racers in New England. A special series of racing seminars affords you the opportunity to train with nationally ranked skiers.

SAFETY: The trails are patrolled during the day, and all groomed trails are swept at the close of operations.

CHILDCARE FACILITIES: None.

CONNECTED TO THE CATAMOUNT TRAIL: Yes.

Gestalt: The Trapp Family Lodge Cross Country Touring Center is probably the most renowned facility of its kind in the United States. What other cross country center proprietors have had an Academy Award-winning motion picture made of their life story? How can you resist skiing at the place where Julie Andrews finally settled down after her harrowing escape from the Nazis?

You may hear some nasty criticism of Trapps' from time to time, but don't be fooled—it's fueled by jealousy. Trapps' does live up to its reputation, and it is constantly striving to improve. It offers something for everyone, and you will always find a comfortable mix of Lycra-suited elite racers, stylishly clad guests of the hotel, and neophytes in dungarees.

All intermediate skiers who look at the Trapp trail map for the first time want to make Slayton Pasture Cabin their food-break destination. The cabin gives meaning to the word "rustic." It's a just-what-you-would-like-it-to-look-like log cabin, heated by a just-what-you-would-like-it-to-look-like stone fireplace. To add to the legend, the person who cooks the food actually lives there—sans electricity, running water, and "Arsenio Hall." Supplies are delivered by snowmobile. Unfortunately, this fantasy is not within the reach of all who set out on the path. The cabin is 5 km from the ski lodge, mainly up. We have passed more than one group who have abandoned their pursuit of this appealing rustic ambience.

Nevertheless, the cabin sits in the hub of recommended trails for intermediate and advanced skiers. Intermediates should approach the cabin on Sugar Road and Cabin Trail and return to the lodge via Haul Road. Advanced skiers will enjoy the downhill runs on Parizo Trails. If you're an advanced wilderness skier, the trek from Slayton Cabin along Skytop Trail, returning via Skytop or Burt and Ranch Camp Trails, is terrific.

Beginners are also welcome. Try Sugar Road and Russell Knoll Trail to Picnic Knoll, then return via Sugar Road and Fox Track. If you can handle a few more downhill thrills, try Deer Pond or The Sleigh Road.

Trapps' offers a beautiful, clear, Alpine-style trail map with one major flaw: the degree of difficulty of each trail is not noted.

Extras:

RACES: Winter Carnival Race (15 km) in January, informal weekly races, and from time to time, major collegiate and world-class races.

OTHER: For guests of the hotel, there are hot tubs, saunas, an indoor swimming pool, and an exercise facility (with massage).

**Travel
Instructions:**

FROM BOSTON: From I-93 north to I-89 north, exit 10 (Waterbury), take Route 100 north 10 miles. Follow the signs to the Trapp Family Lodge.

FROM NEW YORK: Take I-91 north to I-89 north and proceed as outlined above.

The roads to Stowe are usually well maintained and plowed during snowstorms.

31

Viking Ski Touring Centre

LITTLE POND ROAD
LONDONDERRY, VERMONT 05148

**For Ski
Conditions:**

HOURS OF OPERATION: 8:30 A.M. to 4:30 P.M., daily

SNOW PHONE: 802/824-3933

Profile:

TRAILS: Viking has 20 trails, totaling approximately 40 km, 30 km of which are groomed and track set. An untracked 10-km trail connects the XC center with the village of Weston (part of the trail is shared by snow-mobilers). The trail system is classified as 30 percent easy, 60 percent more difficult, and 10 percent most difficult.

GROOMING: Above average. Although Viking does not use state-of-the-art grooming equipment, in 1986–87 they acquired machinery that can create a skiable surface during icy conditions.

RENTALS: Viking rents Trak and Rossignol waxless skis, SNS bindings, and Salomon boots. They also rent a few pairs of waxable skis and snowshoes.

FOR WAX LOVERS: A complete supply of wax accessories is available. There is a wood-stove-heated area set aside for waxing.

FOOD & LODGING: Viking is situated in the middle of a string of Alpine ski areas, each of which is surrounded by restaurants, inns, bed-and-breakfasts, and rental condominiums.

The closest village is Londonderry, a typically picturesque New England town that has a variety of worthwhile inns and restaurants. The restaurant to try in Londonderry is at the Three Clock Inn, where reservations are a must.

However, our favorite eating and sleeping spots are in the village of Jamaica, some 20 miles away, on Route 30. In Jamaica we have had many fine meals at both the Three Mountain Inn and the Jamaica House, each of which offers reasonably priced accommodations.

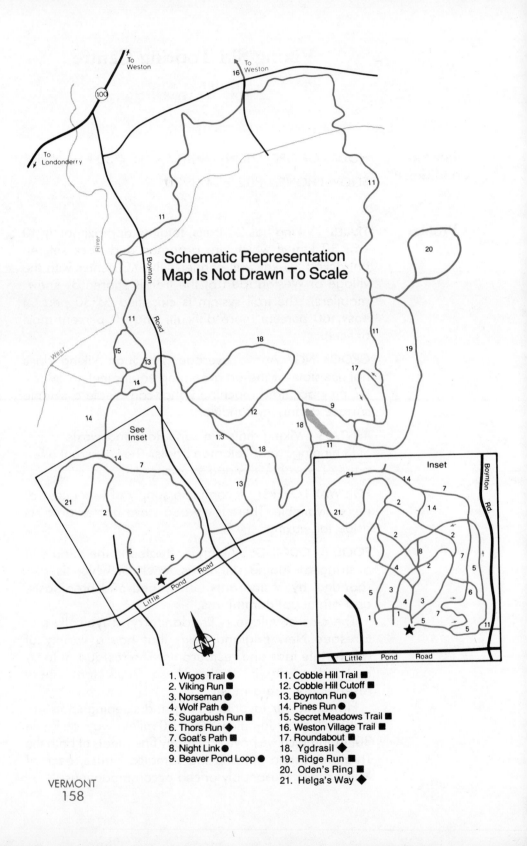

Schematic Representation
Map Is Not Drawn To Scale

1. Wigos Trail ●
2. Viking Run ■
3. Norseman ●
4. Wolf Path ●
5. Sugarbush Run ■
6. Thors Run ◆
7. Goat's Path ■
8. Night Link ●
9. Beaver Pond Loop ●
10.
11. Cobble Hill Trail ■
12. Cobble Hill Cutoff ■
13. Boynton Run ●
14. Pines Run ●
15. Secret Meadows Trail ■
16. Weston Village Trail ■
17. Roundabout ■
18. Ygdrasil ◆
19. Ridge Run ■
20. Oden's Ring ■
21. Helga's Way ◆

The ski center also houses a small café and has three rooms (with breakfast) available for rent.

ALPINE FACILITIES IN AREA: Stratton Mountain, Bromley Mountain, Magic Mountain.

LESSONS: Instruction is available in all methods of cross country skiing.

SAFETY: Viking has both regular ski patrols and end-of-the-day trail sweeps.

CHILDCARE FACILITIES: None.

CONNECTED TO THE CATAMOUNT TRAIL: No.

Gestalt: Viking is one of the oldest cross country ski centers in New England, and in some ways the trail system reminds us of colonial Boston. There is a jumbled inner-city-like area that is a hodgepodge of intersecting trails, mostly of the easy variety; across the road, a Cambridge-like group of trails is mostly rolling, intermediate terrain; and the rural area, the 12-km Cobble Hill Trail, is also undulating, intermediate fare.

The Cobble Hill Trail is the key to the whole system. When this trail is open, it entices intermediate and advanced skiers away from the "inner-city" area, spreads them out, and separates skiers of different abilities. When it is closed, there is grid-lock in inner-city.

Nevertheless, the whole Cobble Hill Trail does not have to be open for Viking to have something to offer advanced and intermediate skiers. Try the following loop: Sugarbush, Cobble Hill, Ridge Run, Wimperdog, Beaver Pond Loop, The Chute (most difficult downhill) or Roundabout (intermediate), Boynton Run, Pines Run, Cobble Hill, Viking Run, and Wolf Path back to the lodge.

Extras: SPECIAL EVENTS: Viking sponsors waxing clinics, guided inn-to-inn tours, races, and moonlight ski tours.

Travel Instructions: FROM BOSTON: Take Route 2 west to I-91 north. Exit at Route 103 north (the Calvin Coolidge Memorial Highway) and head for the town of Chester and Route 11. Take Route 11 west; Viking is past North Windham, on the right.

FROM NEW YORK: Take I-91 north to Route 103. Proceed as outlined above.

These roads are usually well maintained.

32

Woodstock Ski Touring Center

ROUTE 106
WOODSTOCK, VERMONT 05091

For Ski Conditions:

HOURS OF OPERATION: 9:00 A.M. to dusk, daily

SNOW PHONE: 802/457-2114
                           802/457-1100, ext. 274

Profile:

TRAILS: Woodstock has 34 trails, totaling approximately 70 km, which include 20 km of unpatrolled wilderness. They groom and double-track set 50 km of the trails, as needed; it requires 10 hours to track set the entire system. Skating is available on the golf course and on certain trails in the Mt. Tom and Mt. Peg systems. Of the groomed trails, 30 percent are classified as easy, 60 percent more difficult, and 10 percent most difficult.

GROOMING: Above average to excellent. Woodstock uses state-of-the-art grooming equipment. The overall quality of their grooming is only diminished when compared to the top five ski areas.

RENTALS: Woodstock rents Fischer waxless and waxable skis, all of which are mounted with Salomon (SNS) bindings matched by Salomon boots. They also have a few pairs of skating skis and five pairs of snowshoes.

FOR WAX LOVERS: A complete selection of wax accessories is available. Waxing is permitted in the wood-stove-heated sun-room.

FOOD & LODGING: The XC center headquarters is located in the golf facility of the Woodstock Inn, one of the internationally renowned Laurance S. Rockefeller resorts. Although snacks are sold in the ski shop, more substantial fare is available on the second floor in the restaurant/bar, which comes complete with a roaring fireplace and a view of Mount Peg.

The best food on the trail network can be found at the Courtside restaurant, located in the Indoor Sports Center.

Well-manicured Woodstock is commonly regarded as one of New England's most charming villages. There is

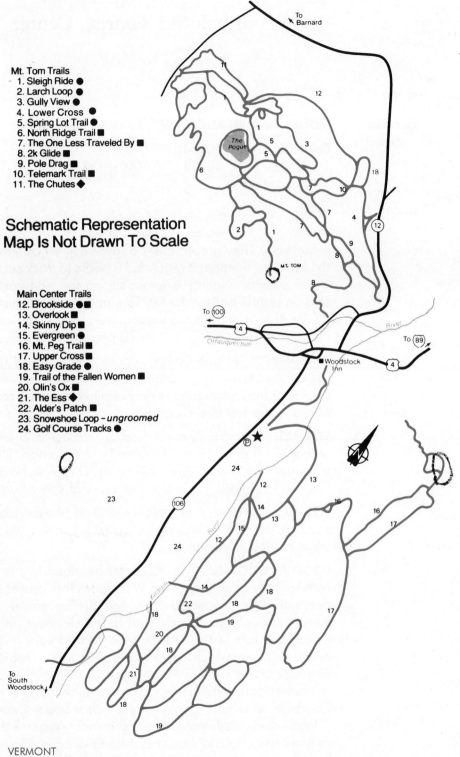

Mt. Tom Trails
1. Sleigh Ride ●
2. Larch Loop ●
3. Gully View ●
4. Lower Cross ●
5. Spring Lot Trail ●
6. North Ridge Trail ■
7. The One Less Traveled By ■
8. 2k Glide ■
9. Pole Drag ■
10. Telemark Trail ■
11. The Chutes ◆

Schematic Representation
Map Is Not Drawn To Scale

Main Center Trails
12. Brookside ●■
13. Overlook ■
14. Skinny Dip ■
15. Evergreen ●
16. Mt. Peg Trail ■
17. Upper Cross ■
18. Easy Grade ●
19. Trail of the Fallen Women ■
20. Olin's Ox ■
21. The Ess ◆
22. Alder's Patch ■
23. Snowshoe Loop – *ungroomed*
24. Golf Course Tracks ●

money here, and sometimes one gets the feeling that one is walking through a set designed for Disneyland.

The town boasts many inns and guesthouses, the queen of which is the Woodstock Inn. On Saturday nights, try the Inn's opulent buffet—it's a far cry from the "steam table fare" that the word buffet usually implies. There are also numerous other places to dine. Our favorite is Bentley's—a Greenwich Village-style coffeehouse, located smack in the middle of Woodstock—which offers a wide range of dinners and snacks.

ALPINE FACILITIES IN AREA: Suicide Six, Killington.

LESSONS: Instruction is available in all methods of cross country skiing.

SAFETY: The trails are patrolled during the day, but there are no trail sweeps at the end of the day.

CHILDCARE FACILITIES: A list of baby-sitters is available.

CONNECTED TO THE CATAMOUNT TRAIL: No.

Gestalt:

The entire Woodstock experience (the town, the restaurants, the inns, and the ski trails) can be one of the most delightful New England ski excursions.

The Woodstock trail system is actually made up of two systems—one on Mount Peg and one on Mount Tom (adjacent to the first Alpine towrope in America). Many of the peaks and vistas are accessible to any skier in reasonably good shape, regardless of ability, because the system provides different ways to get back down the mountain so that skiers can choose downhill runs to match their abilities.

Our favorite sojourn at Woodstock is a day on Mount Tom. To get to the starting point, you must leave the ski center, drive up Route 106 through the center of town, pick up Route 12 north, and continue for a few minutes until you reach Prosper Road. Make a left on Prosper Road, and in a few minutes you will arrive at a small parking area that marks the entrance to the Mount Tom Trail system.

Warm up by taking Sleigh Ride to Gully View. Go left on Gully View up to The Chutes, the most difficult downhill run on Mount Tom. Go down The Chutes, savoring the three hairpin turns, and ski over to North

Run. Go right on North Run, a rolling, predominantly downhill trail that terminates at the old Mount Tom Ski Area (no longer active). Pick up Telemark Trail and head for Spring Lot Trail. If you are a telemarker, you may be tempted to try some linked turns on old Mount Tom. Take Spring Lot back to Gully View. Make a right turn on Gully View and head up to the recently built heated log cabin, a great spot for picnics. Then ski for the Pogue via Sleigh Ride. At the Pogue, a small frozen pond, there are a couple of benches and a lot of peacefulness.

The Pogue is another perfect spot for a lunch break or a check on energy levels. If you're tired, head back to the car via Sleigh Ride. If you're still interested in some ups and downs, take Sleigh Ride to North Ridge Trail, which will eventually lead you back to the parking area, but not until you have experienced one of the best views in Woodstock and negotiated a downhill run that features six hairpin turns.

The best vista in the system is from the top of Mount Peg, a trek for advanced and intermediate skiers. Skiing the perimeter trails is probably the least confusing way to the top (always turn right), and skiing down Mount Peg Trail and Overlook is certainly the most joyful way back to the bottom.

Applause for the trail map, please—one of the best. The ski center now provides an accurate contour map that presents lots of information—including scenic descriptions of each trail.

Extras: RACES: Woodstock annually hosts a 15-km race on the first Saturday in January.

OTHER: There are many pleasantries available in Woodstock. To begin with, the ski center (in summer, a golf clubhouse) includes plush locker rooms, where you can take a hot shower after a hard day's ski. There is also a very plush sports center at the far end of the golf course that is open to the public and features tennis, squash, swimming, a weight room, sauna, and Jacuzzi.

Travel Instructions:

FROM BOSTON: Follow I-93 north to I-89 north, exit 1. Take Route 4 west to the center of Woodstock, turn left on Route 106 south, drive past the Woodstock Inn, and in two minutes the ski center will be on your left.

FROM NEW YORK: Take I-91 north to exit 9. Go left on Route 5 for one mile, then go left on Route 12 for approximately five miles to Route 4 west. Proceed as outlined above.

The roads to Woodstock are usually well maintained and plowed during snowstorms.